ACQUISITIONS

ALA Neal-Schuman purchases fund advocacy,
awareness, and accreditation programs
for library professionals worldwide.

ACQUISITIONS
Core Concepts and Practices

SECOND EDITION

JESSE HOLDEN

An imprint of the American Library Association

Chicago   2017

JESSE HOLDEN is an Account Services Manager for EBSCO Information Services and the former Head of Acquisitions at the University of Southern California. He is an instructor for the ALCTS "Fundamentals of Electronic Resource Acquisitions" online course, a previous instructor for the "Fundamentals of Acquisitions" course, and has been editor of the column "Acquisitions Archaeology" in the journal *Against the Grain*. He earned his MLIS at San Jose State University.

© 2017 by Jesse Holden

Extensive effort has gone into ensuring the reliability of the information in this book; however, the publisher makes no warranty, express or implied, with respect to the material contained herein.

ISBNs
978-0-8389-1460-1 (paper)
978-0-8389-1491-5 (PDF)
978-0-8389-1492-2 (ePub)
978-0-8389-1493-9 (Kindle)

Library of Congress Cataloging-in-Publication Data

Names: Holden, Jesse, author.
Title: Acquisitions : core concepts and practices / by Jesse Holden.
Other titles: Acquisitions in the new information universe
Description: Second edition. | Chicago : ALA Neal-Schuman, an imprint of the American
    Library Association, 2017. | Revision of: Acquisitions in the new information universe : core
    competencies and ethical practices / Jesse Holden. New York : Neal-Schuman Publishers,
    c2010. | Includes bibliographical references and index.
Identifiers: LCCN 2016026852 | ISBN 9780838914601 (print : alk. paper) | ISBN
    9780838914915 (pdf) | ISBN 9780838914922 (epub) | ISBN 9780838914939 (kindle)
Subjects: LCSH: Acquisitions (Libraries) | Acquisition of electronic information resources. |
    Libraries and electronic publishing. | Acquisitions (Libraries)—Technological innovations. |
    Acquisitions (Libraries)—Philosophy. | Acquisitions librarians—Professional ethics.
Classification: LCC Z689 .H74 2016 | DDC 025.2—dc23 LC record available at https://lccn.loc
    .gov/2016026852

Cover design by Kim Thornton. Image © Jannis Tobias Werner/Shutterstock, Inc.

Design and composition by Dianne M. Rooney in the Electra LH and Univers typefaces.

♾ This paper meets the requirements of ANSI/NISO Z39.48–1992 (Permanence of Paper).

Printed in the United States of America

21 20 19 18 17   5 4 3 2 1

This book is dedicated
to my acquisitions mentors

Kittie Henderson,
Carol Lawrence,
Sharon Propas, and
Regina Wallen.

Contents

APPENDIX

We live in a world where there is more and more information, and less and less meaning.

—Jean Baudrillard, *Similacra and Simulation*

Preface to the Second Edition

It is generally known that librarians, as members of a practice-oriented profession, harbor a reluctance—if not an outright reticence—to engage with theory. Throughout the profession, there is a general but genuine aversion to the "T" word. It is my long-held belief, however, that librarianship owes as much to theory as other professions—teaching or lawyering, for example. It was with this perspective that I set about several years ago to develop a theory-based, concept-oriented approach to acquisitions.

Shortly after *Acquisitions in the New Information Universe: Core Competencies and Ethical Practices* was published in 2010, I came across Manuel DeLanda's slim but significant treatise *A New Philosophy of Society: Assemblage Theory and Social Complexity*. While DeLanda's theory (which in turn had been adapted from the more abstract philosophy of Gilles Deleuze) does not deal with librarianship, a lightbulb went on for me nonetheless. While I had cobbled together what seemed to me an adequate theoretical approach to acquisitions in the first edition of *Acquisitions*, DeLanda's "Assemblage Theory" better described and more thoroughly elaborated what I had wanted to say about acquisitions. Assemblage Theory makes it possible to unify the heterogeneous, sometimes disparate components of acquisitions in a logical and scalable way. It was, in short, the very theory I had been searching for.

Two other events more or less coincided with the publication of the first edition. The first was the launch of Web-scale "discovery services" that changed how librarians and library users search for and connect with content. The second event was the growing impact of global economic crisis. By 2010, it had become abundantly clear that this crisis would have a significant and, most importantly, lasting on impact library budgets. The profound changes in the technological and economic environments coupled with the serendipitous discovery of DeLanda's Assemblage Theory led me to the conclusion that a second edition would not only be essential to address abrupt and drastic changes within libraries, but would provide the opportunity to expand my discussion about several core aspects of acquisitions as well.

The approach that I take in the following text has been abstracted from real-world practice and, as such, is fully intended to be a practical work. However, as a *concept-driven* book, it is organized by *strategic assemblages* rather than the perhaps more familiar discrete, linear processes that would constitute a "how-to" guide. My goal is to provide a means of comprehensively structuring acquisitions as professional endeavor.

The text has been completely revised throughout and significantly expanded. The result is a text about acquisitions that is more expansive, coherent, and theoretically robust.

Acknowledgments

Second chances are hard to come by. I am grateful to ALA Editions for the opportunity to revise and expand this book at a time when so much is changing. I would especially like to thank my editor, Jamie Santoro, who has infused this project with positive energy and great ideas—and kept everything on track. Managing editor Angela Gwizdala and copyeditor Tim Johnson worked diligently to guide the manuscript through to publication. I would also like to acknowledge the extremely talented Kim Thornton for her splendid cover design.

Early revisions benefited greatly from review by John McDonald, Associate Dean for Collections at the University of Southern California, and Martin Garner, Dean of the Library at the University of Colorado Colorado Springs and former chair of ALA's Committee on Professional Ethics (COPE). I sincerely appreciate their willingness to provide valuable feedback regarding the changes to this new edition.

My perspective on acquisitions has been greatly enriched since I wrote the first edition. I have had the opportunity to work with the dedicated acquisitions staff at the University of Southern California. I would especially like to acknowledge the Director of Technical Services, Wayne Shoaf, for his support, and the acquisitions section mangers with whom I collaborated on a daily basis: Diana Hayes, Mary Ella Hemmert, Lana Litvan, and Shannon Mansion. I also appreciated the ongoing dialog with the subject selectors concerning the development of the collections.

I have learned a great deal about the "other" side of acquisitions since joining EBSCO. My fellow Account Service Managers have been extremely generous in sharing their collective expertise and helping me adjust to a whole new perspective on the library world. I am especially thankful for the support of Marsha Aucoin, my ASM Team Manager, and Lisa Lombardo, Senior Manager of Customer Success.

Last but definitely not least, I would like to thank my wife, Elizabeth, and children, Elliot and Adelaide, who were supportive of this project even though it took time away from them. Elliot, especially, conscientiously kept me focused when other distractions arose—thank you, Buddy!

CHAPTER **ONE**

Acquisitions
An Overview

W hile the passage of time has tempered enthusiasm for the widespread use of novel technologies (including microfilm, CD-ROMs, the Internet and World Wide Web, mobile devices, etc.) and experience has diminished people's expectations for these always-already-obsolescing technologies, it is an undeniable truism that information technology has had a profound, often revolutionary, and ever-accelerating impact on how we think and communicate. The evolving practices within the contemporary **information ecosystem** continue to fundamentally change the way people conceive of and engage with information. While various applications and adaptations of technology have not been utopian by any means, acceleration of technology-based access to information has delivered a significant amount of change in a relatively short time.

The library, as a dynamic hub of social and cultural communication, continues to undergo profound changes. These transformative changes have affected not only information but the entire information environment (Pritchard, 2008). As an important nexus within its respective ecology, the library functions as both a lens through which changes in the wider ecosystem may be examined and also a mirror in which these changes are constantly reflected. If the library, then, is an apparatus *in* and *through* which the constant changes in this "age of information" can be examined, it is essential that the contemporary information professional fully understands the role that the library now plays—as well as the potential future roles it will likely play. Within each individual library, it is imperative that those individuals who source, purchase, and secure access to selected information—that is, those professionals who practice acquisitions—are fully aware of the complexities that impact the production, distribution, and, especially, access within the respective information ecosystem(s).

Five concepts are particularly important to clarify before beginning a more focused discussion of acquisitions. An acquisitions professional will need to be conscious of:

- Information
- Content
- Format
- Access
- Feedback

While the latter three terms will be addressed in later chapters, an initial clarification between the respective *idea of* as well as the *distinction between* "information" and "content" is essential for establishing a meaningful discussion. The difference between these two terms has become blurred in the shift to the Information Age.

Information Paradigm

As **information** and **content** become synonymous in popular usage, they also lose their respective meanings. In the following pages, these terms will be used in different (and deliberate) ways.

Within the context of libraries, and acquisitions in particular, we are concerned both with what can be *known* (i.e., information in the most general sense) and what can be *communicated*. While communicability is not necessarily inherent to information, communicable information is obviously necessary for any library-based information practice. Any information that can be communicated can also be contained—most generally in a language, but also in a book, a database, a video, etc. Therefore, this class of information that can be communicated will henceforth be referred to as "content." The distinction between information and content will be important in the discussion that follows because it is a refutation of some contemporary ideas about the nature of information. One persistent idea concerning information is that it is ethereal—all around us, yet not tangible—and therefore "free." For example, Electronic Frontier Foundation (EFF) cofounder John Perry Barlow has asserted that information "isn't a noun," "a thing," or "an object" (Barlow, 2008: xvi). However, a case can be made for the materiality inherent in any discrete piece of information or "information object" (see chapter 3).

Our discourse about the value of information, our social and economic dependence on it, the sheer abundance of it, and, not least of all, our professional engagement with it contributes to our information **paradigm**, or the coherent system of thought and perception in which we understand and use information. To situate acquisitions in this paradigm—that is, within the Information Age—we must begin with a simple question: What is information? In the context of following discussion, the answer is the simplest one: information can be almost anything. Information at this most basic level is anything that can be known. In light of this very general definition, it is worth keeping in mind that the hallmark of this age is abundance—and presumed availability—of information. And along with the presumption of availability is the accompanying assumption that any of this information can be accessed anytime from anywhere it is needed. The vast production and rapid communication of information that underlies this paradigm does not always imply a corresponding increase in quality (e.g., clarity, accuracy, etc.) or meaning (e.g., relevance, usefulness, etc.). It has become a truism that more seldom equals better. Because of that, any work with information becomes ever more complex, contextualized, and specialized.

So what does it mean to work within the **Information Age**? To situate acquisitions practice (as described below)—indeed, all library practices—within this information age the term must be more clearly defined. "Age" here does not refer to the geological time period (e.g., Ice Age) but to a socio-historical one (e.g., the Gilded Age or the Middle Ages). The concept of an "age" is useful because the term encapsulates a unique paradigm, or a coherent system of thought and perception. In the Middle Ages, for example, a peasant might have expected to travel no more than a few miles from his or her birthplace. In the Information Age, on the other hand, an information professional might expect to be connected to a globalized network via mobile computing devices. While in many cases the precise boundary of an age may seem somewhat debatable (or even entirely arbitrary), such a designation is not merely a way to break up the continuum of time for the convenience of study.

Such a conception of change as successive, independent historical frames is informed by two important concepts. The first of these concepts is Michel Foucault's "archaeological" perspective of history. Encapsulated within each temporal frame of reference, or "stratum," is a particular discourse—that is, paradigm—which follows the logic intrinsic to that stratum. This resulting temporal stratum or "age" is marked off by "a profound breach in the expanse of continuities" (Foucault, 1994: 217), the moment when that internal logic suddenly changes. In a second, related concept, Thomas Kuhn (1996) describes "paradigm shift," which he famously used to explain the progression of scientific revolutions. Rather than conceiving of scientific thought as changing in a gradual, even manner through the course of history, Kuhn postulates that a shift in paradigm is the result of an acute crisis—specifically, the inability of a former, accepted paradigm to explain what is being observed. At the point an established paradigm loses its explanatory power, a new paradigm must be defined to fully account for the emergent anomalies.

These changes do not necessarily mark "progress" as such. Library practice in the Information Age is just one example of contemporary discourses arranged according to a relative logic that is different from the discourse of a preceding age. (Librarianship in the present age differs markedly from, say, librarianship of the Middle Ages.) However, it is also important to note that our current discourse of library practice is also distinct from other discourses of the age (such as publishing or technology), though it overlaps or is related to many such discourses. Therefore, when constructing a model for acquisitions, contemporary librarianship must center on electronic information and mobile devices—even though these relatively new technologies do not fully describe the paradigm of our information age. Content is produced and distributed in many forms and formats. Practices developed in the Print Age are no longer adequate to fully account for library needs of today, but will continue to inform our practices into the future. The real key for the successful acquisitions practitioner is to fully grasp all the array of content that is available.

Identifying and contextualizing the paradigm of library practice is important as acquisitions professionals evaluate services and workflows, many of which are built upon legacy practices. When reviewing and developing acquisitions services and workflows, it must be *specific to* and *contained in* the paradigm of the age in which it emerges. Following Kuhn's logic, this age is *contiguous to* but not always *continuous with* the preceding age. If the information ecosystem has been set apart by a recent shift (rather than a gradual evolution), the question becomes: what does this mean for acquisitions practice? That is, what does it mean to say we "do acquisitions"? First and foremost, it means that in managing acquisitions, services and workflows must be premised on and built around present needs rather than past practices. Instead of incrementally adjusting legacy policies and procedures, often entire approaches to acquiring information must be rethought and implemented anew.

What Is a Collection?

Before defining acquisitions and its associated competencies, it is essential to understand the changing library **collection**. Libraries are dynamic, multifaceted hubs of information transmission. Whether conceived as physical or virtual spaces (or both), people think of libraries as fulfilling any number of roles. Some think of the library in terms of quality programming, such as story hours or archival exhibits. Others may think more in terms of valuable facilities, such as meeting spaces and computer labs. Still others may think of services, such as job fairs or research assistance. However, what stands out about libraries to most people are the collections—those masses of information resources that communities depend on libraries for. Library collections are depended upon for local resources—such as genealogies and local histories, as well as content with a broader scope—such as a wide variety of languages or formats.

Lee (2000: 1111), for example, making note of the changing nature of what constitutes a *collection*, has suggested that "given the new reality . . . it would be beneficial to broaden the concept of the collection to reflect the continuity and interconnectivity characteristic" of the contemporary information environment. For Lee, like many librarians, the idea of the collection cannot necessarily be conveniently defined or limited by what is "owned" (see chapter 2). **Collection development** is the formal, professional function of "developing the collection"—that is, using subject expertise and knowledge of the library's user community to select content available to users. This selection includes content in the library's traditional physical collection, but it has also come to encompass the entire sphere of access provided by the library.

Rick Anderson (2006) has gone so far as to suggest moving away from a permanent just-in-case collection in favor of just-in-time acquisitions in those cases where such a model better meets library user needs; he has emphasized the possibility to reorganize collection development around the emerging ability to respond to library user demand by "showing our patrons everything that's available and buying only what they need" (2009: 86). Clearly the idea of access to content that is driven primarily—or even entirely—by real-time demand is significant for the practice of acquisitions, as it signals an important shift from building a general collection, a linear process, to more precisely meeting specific needs at the point they arise, something altogether different and much less straightforward. In the ontological realignment that underpins the whole paradigm shift, even the priority of the collection within the library's organization scheme, long taken for granted, is fundamentally called into question.

Though the concept of "the collection" is practically metonymic with the library, our idea of *collection* has become more expansive, complicated, and ambiguous—in a sense, more fluid—with every new publication and every new format. This is especially true with increased production of content being distributed in electronic media, consistent with the just-in-time paradigm described above (see chapter 2, "Assemblages of Access"). Despite the ever-expanding notion of library collections, "the book" remains a powerful symbol—indeed, another metonym—of the library for many of its users.

What Is Acquisitions?

So, what is **acquisitions**?

Though perceived, perhaps, as merely "buying books," acquisitions is an increasingly complicated sub-profession of librarianship that encompasses the "business side" of collection development. It is the flip side of the collection-building coin. While collection development focuses primarily on selection, acquisitions makes that selected, paid-for content available to authorized uses. Often taken for granted within the context of the larger library endeavor, *acquisitions* is at once the most obvious and often least understood function both within the library (understood either as a place or service) and within librarianship. While most people intuit that one or more professionals within a library select those resources to which the library provides access, rarely is much thought given to the process by which this takes place.

Acquisitions is composed of several interrelated core competencies. These competencies encompass the typical responsibilities (and corresponding skills) required by acquisitions librarians, managers, and staff to organize and practice their profession. Previous approaches to identifying competencies have identified various ways to list and group those related to acquisitions (Fisher, 2001). In contemporary practice, "technological and organizational changes make it challenging to define a set of specific competencies" within any area of collection management, including acquisitions (Martin and Zaghloul, 2011: 313). However, in the following discussion, competencies will be grouped into four main organizationally based groups: ordering, receiving, establishing access, and paying. These four competency groups comprise the acquisitions assemblage—the general organizational components required to acquire content for the library; while these competencies are consistent across organizations, the actual distribution of tasks within respective contexts may vary considerably.

A contemporary organizational approach to acquisitions may take a cue from the substantial effort put toward the Functional Requirements for Bibliographic Records (FRBR) model developed within the cataloging community. This "conceptual model for the bibliographic universe"

ACQUISITIONS CORE COMPETENCIES

Ordering	Establishing Access
Receiving	Paying

(Tillett, 2004) generalizes bibliographic entities, their creators, and the relationship between the two. This model has generated significant debate in the profession and has profound implications for restructuring both the approach to and practice of cataloging. Though the outcomes of this discussion are far from certain, the concepts and the conversation has nonetheless informed a kind of reflexive reevaluation of the purpose and practice of cataloging. As the changing nature of information production and its subsequent communication have precipitated a reevaluation of the idea of cataloging practice, so too should it likewise affect the approach to and practice of the acquisition of library content. What we see within librarianship is the shift from a modern to a truly postmodern praxis that must be marked by a simultaneous change in thought as well as practice.

Of course, the Web—and cloud-based services in particular—is the primary driver behind this change and, as such, it is easy to see the networked environment as either a panacea or pariah. But this is not to say that everything that matters is available online, nor to advocate that it should be. This is likewise not to suggest that physical materials across a variety of media are no longer relevant or should no longer be considered content for use by and within a particular user community. However, when looking at *information* specifically as *content* within a library context and how it is handled by acquisitions, what becomes critical in the execution and evaluation of practice is the premise that the Web is a de facto part of the environment, along with other formats, rather than an afterthought or a supplement. The implication for practice in an information ecosystem comprised of online and other digital media is that any practices must necessarily be built with the understanding that online media will be a critical part of that environment.

As noted above, the notion of what constitutes a collection has become rather fluid. One of the undeniable trends of the Internet Age is the increased sensitivity to access. "Access" may be defined broadly as the ability to consume specific information, but should not necessarily be constrained by a notion of immediacy. In other words, access is best interpreted broadly: it does not mean that everything need be immediately accessible on demand or that all demands for content must be immediately filled. The issues surrounding access have burgeoned from the straightforward act of finding information to the more nuanced and complicated contemporary regime of copyright, so-called "digital rights management"

(DRM), and the sheer amount of information, useful or not, that can be retrieved from even the most basic of Web searches. The overwhelming intricacies of access in the rapidly maturing Information Age have necessarily repositioned the information professional well within this regime.

It would be a mistake, however, to approach twenty-first-century acquisitions from the point of view of access alone. Though it was recognized some time ago that "acquisitions will be redefined in terms of access" (Gorman, 1997: xiii, paraphrasing Cornish, 1997), only recently is it becoming clear exactly what that means. Cornish (1997), for his part, conceives of access in terms of how content is funded by the library rather than how it is collected for use. In Cornish's approach, content should only be acquired if it is within the scope of a given collection. What has emerged since this model was put forward is a regime in which the line between what exactly is or is not the library collection can be difficult to draw definitively.

Why Theory?

Librarianship, as a user-centered, service profession, often gets caught up in immediate tasks related to meeting user needs. A practical focus on providing information, maintaining facilities, evaluating staff, talking to colleagues, and acquiring content (among many other demands) frequently defines the daily work of librarians.

So, why "theory"?

In the effort to meet the tangible needs of users in any given community, it is often forgotten that the professional work of librarians is more than the sum of the tasks they complete or statistics they report. "Theory" in this context just means a unified way of describing, organizing, and planning the work. Theory allows for the strategic and synthetic thinking that makes a profession a profession. Theory need not be complicated; however, a theory that merely describes is less useful than one that explains. In practicing a profession, detailed observation is not enough. To properly engage with the profession, strategic planning and efficient execution are essential. Therefore, identifying and employing a relevant theory is an integral part of being an acquisitions professional.

To successfully acquire content in the contemporary information environment, a useful theory needs to be both robust and flexible. Manuel DeLanda's "Assemblage Theory" (2006) can be used to organize, synthesize, plan, and execute acquisitions work. The key concept of the theory is that of the eponymous "assemblage." In defining an **assemblage**, DeLanda argues "that a whole may be both analyzable into separate parts and at the same time have irreducible properties, properties that emerge from the interaction between parts" (10). An assemblage is, therefore, more than a mere grouping or categorization—it goes beyond a basic taxonomy of parts in a fixed relation. Instead, Assemblage Theory allows for scalable wholes—that is, assemblages—that are made up of parts that may themselves be wholes—that is, other assemblages. But each respective assemblage is more than the sum of its parts because of the interactions of the parts within it. For example, the profession of "acquisitions" is an assemblage of four main parts—or, in this case, competencies: ordering, receiving, establishing access, and paying. What makes acquisitions an assemblage is that the four competencies are not functioning separately and independently, but rather acquisitions by its nature brings these related processes together so that they are constantly interacting.

The library is an example of an assemblage. This assemblage can be thought of in very simple terms. While the library is conceptually a single unified, entity—something that is fundamentally irreducible—it is also made up of many separate and recognizable parts. For example, public services, technical services, and administration are all organizational components—that is, separate parts—of the library. These separate parts, in turn, are assemblages of their own, constituted of other separate, irreducible components (see chapter 2). At the same time, the library is more than just a random group of loosely associated organizational components. These components each contribute something unique organizationally, but also interact and, significantly, integrate with each other to constitute the distinct entity that we know as the library. Going in the other direction, the library itself is a component in even larger assemblages: organizationally, the library may be part of a municipal or university assemblage; conceptually, the library may be part of the more abstract assemblage of librarianship.

Why Ethics?

The topic of "**ethics**" comes up frequently in contemporary discourse, and often swirls around day-to-day discussions regarding politics, business, medicine, and law. But ethics actually has a long history. Ethics is one of the main branches of philosophy, and in the Western tradition can be traced back to the ancient Greeks. Thought, discussion, and disagreement about ethics stretch back to the foundation of philosophical thought, and many perspectives about the idea and practice of ethics have been developed over time.

But what does ethics mean, exactly?

Technically, "ethics" is "the philosophical study of morality" (Deigh, 2009: 284). It is inquiry into right and wrong. For our purposes, the term ethics will be used more generally to mean "actions that are right." Formal ethical assemblages may be derived from philosophical tradition, such as the ancient philosophy of Epicurus or the modern "utilitarianism" of John Stuart Mill. Religious teaching may also provide a formal ethical assemblage. A less formal personal approach to ethics, such as using "The Golden Rule" (or "treat others as you wish to be treated"), may also inform an individual's notion of right and wrong (Gensler, 2013). An ethical assemblage may draw from several sources, as well.

Today, public attention is often drawn to situations involving medical ethics or political ethics that appear in the news, especially in cases when there has been a *breach of ethics*—an instance where someone has failed to do what was right. Other kinds of ethics include business ethics, information ethics, and professional ethics. In the context of library practice, ethics can be informed by the law, institutional mission, or professional codes.

While philosophers have spent centuries debating the nature of "right"—such as where right derives from and what right means—in the context of acquisitions there are some guidelines that can keep daily practice and organizational policy on an ethical track. Ethical actions may include:

1. dealing honestly (with colleagues, users, and vendors),
2. working efficiently,
3. obeying the law,

4. serving the "customers" (see below),
5. following established collection guidelines,
6. tracking funds accurately,
7. understanding the business of publishing, and
8. acting as a steward for institutional resources.

Librarians strive to be ethical professionals and, as in many other professions, have put together several codes to help guide individuals to do "right actions" in their daily work and interactions. Schuman affirms that "as librarians, we are a **profession** ethically dedicated to the organization and dissemination of information—the dissemination, therefore, of knowledge and power" (1990: 87). And in working with such knowledge and power comes great responsibility.

The stakes of ethical practice are high. Acquisitions professionals may deal with large sums of money, a variety of people, and numerous (not to mention *expensive*) information resources. In their comprehensive *Guide to Ethics in Acquisitions*, vanDuinkerken, Kaspar, and Harrell explain that "the need to develop ethical standards for acquisitions librarians emerged as the concern for the potential misuse of the acquisitions budget increased" (19). Or, to put it simply: "As acquisitions budgets grew, ethical concerns increased" (Ibid., 19–20).

Applying Ethics

Besides the general *functional responsibilities* which form one assemblage within acquisitions practice, the *applied ethics* of acquisitions constitutes another important, closely related assemblage. These two assemblages function in separate but also overlapping ways, and form part of the larger acquisitions assemblage. The ethical component is one upon which any sound assemblage of acquisitions practice must be predicated. Ethics was defined generally in chapter 1 as "actions that are right." More technically, ethics may be a simple "guiding philosophy" or a more comprehensive "theory or system of moral values." Ethics may also be more specifically defined in a professional context as "the principles of conduct governing an individual or a group" (Merriam-Webster Online). Acquisitions practice is multifaceted and its ethical components usually include:

- service,
- business,
- supervision, and/or
- scholarship.

With the shifts in both the informational and economic environments in which acquisitions functions, the understanding, articulation, and practice of ethics within daily work and strategic planning is more crucial than ever. Tightening budgets and increased financial scrutiny coupled with the explosion of available and desirable content requires a deliberate *engagement with* and *discussion about* ethics as they relate to all interactions and transactions. Therefore, ethics, too, may be thought of as an assemblage in its own right, in addition to being part of the acquisitions assemblage.

Applying ethics involves putting a general knowledge into practice. Like implementing a technology (technological practice) or fulfilling an organizational mission (institutional practice), such knowledge can be applied when developing specific competencies. In the case of acquisitions, ethics can be applied when paying an invoice and accounting for expenditures, or interacting with vendors and library colleagues to identify and order content for acquisition. Ethical actions like honesty, fairness, and timeliness may not apply exclusively to acquisitions competencies but are essential components of the acquisitions assemblage.

To facilitate an understanding and application of ethics within library practice, systems of values have been codified within the American Library Association (ALA). ALA's code of ethics was first adopted in 1939 and has undergone many revisions over the years (see the appendix for the full Code of Ethics). While the code recognizes that librarians "significantly influence or control the selection, organization, preservation, and dissemination of information," significantly, acquisitions is not included among the areas of "influence or control." The Code also states that its principles "are expressed in broad statements to guide ethical decision making. These statements provide a framework; they cannot and do not dictate conduct to cover particular situations." As such, no specific provisions are made for acquisitions work. It is also worth noting that the International Federation of Library Associations (IFLA) also has a "Code of Ethics for Librarians and Other Information Workers."

Because of the general nature of ALA's Code, a critical guide for any practitioner of acquisitions is the "Statement on Principles and Standards of Acquisitions Practice" developed by the ALCTS Acquisitions Section Ethics Task Force (see sidebar). While the Statement is not explicitly a code of ethics, and arguably lacks the moral force of the latter (Holden, 2012), it does provide twelve concrete guidelines for "right action" when practicing acquisitions. The Statement is especially useful as a de facto, if somewhat narrow guide for those who are new to acquisitions or just learning the business side of library collections. As vanDuinkerken, Kaspar, and Harrell note: "An acquisitions librarian's reactions to ethical situations vary depending on the specific circumstances. Understanding the twelve guidelines will aid the acquisitions librarian in navigating the ethical waters of their library and profession" (31). However, application of the Statement's guidelines must be executed within a broader ethical context, which should include, at the very least, both the ALA Code and a respective library's code (where one exists).

STATEMENT ON PRINCIPLES AND STANDARDS OF ACQUISITIONS PRACTICE

In all acquisitions transactions, a librarian:

1. gives first consideration to the objectives and policies of his or her institution;
2. strives to obtain the maximum ultimate value of each dollar of expenditure;
3. grants all competing vendors equal consideration insofar as the established policies of his or her library permit, and regards each transaction on its own merits;
4. subscribes to and works for honesty, truth, and fairness in buying and selling, and denounces all forms and manifestations of bribery;
5. declines personal gifts and gratuities;
6. uses only by consent original ideas and designs devised by one vendor for competitive purchasing purposes;
7. accords a prompt and courteous reception insofar as conditions permit to all who call on legitimate business missions;
8. fosters and promotes fair, ethical, and legal trade practices;

9. avoids sharp practice;

10. strives consistently for knowledge of the publishing and book-selling industry;

11. strives to establish practical and efficient methods for the conduct of his/her office;

12. counsels and assists fellow acquisitions librarians in the performance of their duties, whenever occasion permits.

Developed by the ALCTS (Association for Library Collections and Technical Services) Acquisitions Section Ethics Task Force; endorsed by the ALCTS Acquisitions Section and adopted by the ALCTS Board of Directors, Midwinter Meeting, February 7, 1994. (ALCTS, 1994)

The Statement, on one hand, is a prescriptive list that spells out "right actions" within the acquisitions profession. But taken together, the Code also comprises an assemblage that not only lists correct behaviors but that also defines, in a more general way, an approach to the myriad situations that an acquisitions professional might encounter. While it would be impossible to create an exhaustive list of all possible ethical questions someone might face, it is possible, by way of the examples in the Code, to create an ethics assemblage that provides guidance for the various kinds of ethical decisions that one might need to make in the course of their work.

Conclusion: A Call for Radicalization

The information ecosystem is, by its nature, an ever-expanding one. Information and, specifically, content, is being constantly created, reorganized, stored, and disseminated. Underlying the whole production process is communication—the circulation, exchange, and discussion of ideas. Acquisitions plays a fundamental role in both the production and communication of content. The time has passed when those practicing acquisitions can wait for a stack of paper orders and buy a bunch of books. The information environment within which we work seems, at times, hopelessly complicated. Acquisitions, as part of the larger information ecosystem in which it participates, requires a detailed understanding of not just where something is available, but how. Embedded in this understanding are the requisite competencies for dealing with information. At its most basic, acquisitions requires the ordering, receiving, accessing, and paying for selected content. To be truly successful, however, acquisitions requires successfully integrating daily functions in a theoretical and ethical way.

Goldsborough notes that "today, in the Information Age, we typically think of ourselves as uniquely inundated with information" (2002: 15). His suggestion for managing inundation includes automated filtering functions. However, even with the advances in technology-driven information discovery—a process that has, in practice, already become de facto filtering—the importance of human input is still recognized. Marwick maintains that "it is important to note that knowledge management problems can typically not be solved by the deployment of a technology solution alone" (2001: 816). Navigating the information environment is complex in that it requires maximizing resources in a way that simultaneously expands and narrows the available content that is required by an end user by distilling the most useful content from the broadest number of information sources. At once we are dealing with the constant creation of ever more singularities while trying to manage these myriad singular objects through as few flows as possible.

This pull in equal but opposite directions poses a direct challenge to anyone supporting and providing information services. Circumstances require a generalized understanding of the information ecology while demanding an equally nuanced understanding of that ever-increasing species of information objects that can potentially be acquired.

Acquisitions practices have often developed by addressing change in a gradual, evolutionary manner—that is, by accretion—contrary to the nature of paradigm shift. Daily practice and established workflows have often morphed more by adding exceptions within the acquisitions function than from deliberate engagement with the fundamental paradigm shift affecting the entire information ecosystem. Compounding the problem, "acquisitions" work may be separated from "electronic resources"—an increasingly arbitrary distinction. In order to address this shift, tools and techniques must be derived from current needs and opportunities rather than appended to those practices that arose within a previous age. While defying a formal prescription for specific practice, the new frame of reference for finding and delivering content requires a radicalization of approach rather than simply adding or updating particular actions in an already-fixed workflow. Acquisitions workflows and practices built upon this former approach will be more likely to succeed and adapt in the destabilized, changing information environment in which contemporary librarianship is practiced. Overcoming this inertia requires a comprehensive yet flexible conceptual approach that addresses, rather than accommodates, profound changes and inherent uncertainties.

REFERENCES

Anderson, Rick. 2006. "Crazy Idea #274: Just Stop Collecting." *Against the Grain* 18, no. 4: 50–52.

Anderson, Rick. 2009. "Is the Library Collection Too Risky?" *Against the Grain* 21, no. 3: 86.

Barlow, John Perry. 2008. "Foreword." In *Content: Selected Essays on Technology, Creativity, and the Future of the Future* (pp. xv–xxii), by Cory Doctorow. San Francisco: Tachyon.

Cornish, Graham P. 1997. "Electronic Document Delivery Services and Their Impact on Collection Management." In *Collection Management for the 21st Century: A Handbook for Librarians* (pp. 159–172), edited by G. E. Gorman and Ruth H. Miller. Westport, CT: Greenwood Press.

Deigh, John. 2009. "Ethics." In *The Cambridge Dictionary of Philosophy*, 2nd ed. (pp. 284–289), edited by Robert Audi. New York: Cambridge University Press.

DeLanda, Manuel. 2006. *A New Philosophy of Society: Assemblage Theory and Social Complexity*. New York: Continuum Books.

Fisher, William. 2001. "Core Competencies for the Acquisitions Librarian." *Library Collections, Acquisitions, and Technical Services*. 25: 179–190.

Foucault, Michel. 1994. *The Order of Things: An Archaeology of the Human Sciences*. New York: Vintage Books.

Gensler, Harry J. 2013. *Ethics and the Golden Rule*. New York: Routledge.

Goldsborough, Reid. 2002. "Breaking the Information Logjam." *Reading Today* 20, no. 1 (Aug./Sept.): 15.

Gorman, G. E. 1997. "Introduction." In *Collection Management for the 21st Century: A Handbook for Librarians* (pp. ix–xv), edited by G. E. Gorman and Ruth H. Miller. Westport, CT: Greenwood Press.

Holden, Jesse. 2012. "Acquisitions Archaeology—Professional Ethics." *Against the Grain* 24, no. 2: 72–73.

Kuhn, Thomas S. 1996. *The Structure of Scientific Revolutions*, 3rd ed. Chicago: University of Chicago Press.

Lee, Hur-Li. 2000. "What Is a Collection?" *Journal of the American Society for Information Science* 52, no. 12: 1106–1113.

Martin, Jim and Raik Zaghloul. 2011. "Planning for the Acquisition of Information Resources Management Core Competencies." *New Library World* 112, no. 7/8: 313–320.

Marwick, A. D. 2001. "Knowledge Management and Technology." *IBM Systems Journal* 40, no. 4: 814–830.

Pritchard, Sarah M. 2008. "Deconstructing the Library: Reconceptualizing Collections, Spaces and Services." *Journal of Library Administration* 48, no. 2: 219–233.

Schuman, Patricia Glass. 1990. "The Image of Librarians: Substance or Shadow?" *Journal of Academic Librarianship* 16, Iss. 2.

Tillett, Barbara. 2004. *What Is FRBR? A Conceptual Model for the Bibliographic Universe*. Washington, DC: Library of Congress Cataloging Distribution Service. Available: www.loc.gov/cds/downloads/FRBR.PDF (accessed November 23, 2009).

vanDuinkerken, Wyoma, Wendy Arant Kaspar, and Jeanne Harrell. 2014. *Guide to Ethics in Acquisitions*. (ALCTS Acquisitions Guide Series; no. 17.) Chicago: Acquisitions Section of the Association for Library Collections & Technical Services, American Library Association.

Winseck, Dwayne. 2002. "Illusions of Perfect Information and Fantasies of Control in the Information Society." *New Media and Society* 4, no. 1: 93–122.

CHAPTER **TWO**

Assemblages of Access

P erhaps the most fundamental **assemblage** (see chapter 1) when discussing acquisitions is the **collection** (see chapter 1). Collecting materials *for* and *within* libraries has been a basic part of librarianship from the profession's inception. Indeed, libraries have been associated with their physical collections going back to ancient times. The Alexandria library, for example, remains an enduring archetype of a centralized physical (intensely local) yet intellectually diverse (generally global) knowledge base that symbolizes the collections of the previous paradigm. Though often taken for granted in library discourse (and discourse about libraries), the notion of a collection—any collection—underscores the usefulness of a theory—that is, a synthesizing idea (see chapter 1).

As an assemblage, the library's collection is a complex entity. A library's collection, like the library itself, can be conceived of in fairly simple, monolithic terms: *the collection.* As discussed in chapter 1, however, assemblages are not monolithic entities; rather, they are a complex group of components that both interact and fully integrate. A collection assemblage might be constructed any number of ways. Traditionally, the collection might be thought of as all the library-owned materials within the library building. This conception is based on a paradigm of physical resources purchased and carefully maintained in anticipation of possible—though not certain—future use. A properly conceived assemblage, however, is premised on a paradigm that accounts for different intersecting modes of access. This assemblage becomes much more complex, incorporating various formats, access models, and the unique mix of content selected for the local user community. It is important to keep in mind that even for a given library, the collection assemblage is not a fixed, unchanging entity. An assemblage need not be constructed as a rigid structure, but instead can be used in a contingent, even ad hoc manner depending on a number of factors. This corresponds to a more fluid notion of format that can be adopted specifically within an acquisitions workflow as described in chapter 3. Significantly, however, the assemblage is always more (e.g., more integrated, more holistic, etc.) than the mere sum of its constituent parts.

Long defined primarily by their collections, libraries have depended on the process of getting materials into the collection in an organized, efficient way. Yet, despite the obvious necessity of "getting" those objects that constitute the collection, *acquisitions*—both as a noun (i.e., organizational unit within a library) and verb (i.e., a collective set of processes that makes the library collection as it is generally understood possible)—is often taken for granted. When acquisitions is considered, it tends to be misunderstood in both respects—even by other librarians. The business aspects of managing library budgets (see chapter 5), interacting with for-profit vendors, and keeping financial records are all unfamiliar, perhaps even intimidating practices to those librarians who are not engaged with acquisitions work on a daily basis. In an increasingly complex information ecosystem, where the amount of potentially accessible information proliferates, the role that an acquisitions professional plays in the library likewise becomes more complex—specifically in the context of contemporary collection-building.

With the rapid advance of computing technology leading to ubiquitous, globalized, and especially mobile communication tools, all stakeholders involved in recorded communication—including everyone from authors, filmmakers, musicians, and book publishers to content vendors, libraries, and their respective user communities—have faced considerable upheaval in traditional processes. Many libraries have already moved beyond models of acquisitions that are centered primarily on print (Carr, 2008); an emerging norm is the increased focus on e-resources. While sorting out how this shift has affected, and continues to affect, libraries, a basic question needs to be asked: How has this upheaval shaped the functions of acquisitions today in light of an expanding notion of the library collection?

Part of the confusion stems from the position of acquisitions in the library related to other organizational units within the library, as well as its frequent interactions with entities (like publishers and vendors; see below) outside the library and its community of users. On the one hand, acquisitions does not have an equivalent set of national-level rules such as cataloging librarians use to structure their work. This can make it more difficult to define the scope and competencies of acquisitions work. On the other hand, as a "technical service" acquisitions has not traditionally had the same exposure to and interaction with library users as more public-facing library units such as circulation or reference. While, again, the library must necessarily secure access rights to content so that the library users may, in turn, use that content, most users do not give the acquisitions process any thought as long as they are able to find the information that they are seeking. In truth, library users should not have to think about how content is collected and made available, but such a seamless provision of information is becoming increasingly difficult to accomplish since this content is provided through many routes. Additionally, users may have significant experience using library catalogs and discovery services, as well as commercial services for Web searching, music downloading, and video streaming, and so may be frustrated or confused when attempting to use the library collection. Muddled notions regarding mechanisms of content dissemination might lead to the notion that "everything's online" or that "information wants to be free," or even that a single keyword will lead to the best content.

The other part of the confusion comes from the changing nature of acquisitions itself: the tools used, methods employed, content sought, and—not least of all—the access required. Acquisitions practitioners from a previous age would hardly recognize much of what is done in acquisitions today as a matter of routine. Or, rather, they would not recognize *how* it is

SELECTION AND ACQUISITION

How does the selection-to-acquisition process work?

As an example, a library user wants to recommend a title for purchase. Using the library's Web site, the user contacts someone in the acquisitions unit using either a contact e-mail address or an online form. They likely assumed that the acquisitions staff is responsible for making content decisions in addition to ordering and receiving content.

What happens now?

People often expect that acquisitions involves the complete cycle of identifying, selecting, ordering, and paying for the content that library users have access to. But really, content acquisition usually just encompasses the second part of the content development process: the steps that come *after* a selection decision is made. The *assemblage* of acquisitions tasks and processes are usually performed by an individual or unit other than the one doing the selecting.

In the case of a user-initiated request, someone responsible for content decisions would need to review and approve the request regardless of who was first contacted. Those performing a task traditionally regarded as collection development use a number of factors to make the decision to acquire content. Factors likely include the library's collection development policy and its mission, access issues, and available funding. Once collection development has authorized and assigned a funding source (see "**Funds**"), the request will be forwarded to acquisitions to be ordered.

Often, the order will come through to acquisitions with a suggestion of where to buy the content, such as a local bookstore or popular online vendor. While such recommendations can be helpful in the case of rare or other types of difficult-to-obtain content, the acquisitions practitioner is usually in the best position to make sourcing decisions (see "**Vendors**"). A number of factors are involved in deciding from where to source content, including the potential discount, shipping options and costs, and processing services. The evaluation and selection of content suppliers is one of the key strategic functions for acquisitions. While costs are an important factor, it is important that any decision about a vendor takes into account the services available. Such services could include designated representatives, approval plans (see below), standing orders, or anything else that makes the process of acquisitions easier and more efficient. In the same way that collection development makes strategic decisions about what content is appropriate to provide through the library, acquisitions makes analogous decisions about *how* the content is obtained.

done. The paradigm shift from a stable, print-based environment to diverse ecosystem that includes electronic media has created an environment of permanent flux within acquisitions, just as that permanent flux now permeates the whole library. We are well into the postmodern age when "new formats, new economic realities, and new expectations from our communities will ensure that we will be required to change often from now on" (Propas and Reich, 1995: 46). The rise of electronic journal packages, academic eBooks, streaming media, and various associated pricing models for these new cloud-based and Web-delivered resources underscores the instability inherent to the Information Age. The flux within acquisitions is so constant now as to be an integral condition of the work, to such a degree that the goal of the acquisitions function is to reach a kind of equilibrium rather than achieve perpetual stability.

Challenging the notion of a stable and orderly information ecosystem are the contingencies that come along with processing e-resources. Acquisitions practitioners might be involved in reviewing licensing agreements, setting up online access with a publisher, and responding to service outages, in addition to more traditional acquisitions functions. Given the unique nature of many e-content products, associated access management issues can be very time consuming. Because access is so directly tied to the acquisition process, those involved with acquisitions may be more closely tied to ongoing access than ever before. On top of it all, most libraries will need to maintain a simultaneous workflow for print and other physical-format resources as well.

STABILITY VERSUS EQUILIBRIUM

While stability might have seemed a possibility—or even the ultimate goal—in an ecosystem of "fixed" printed content, it is not a realistic goal for the contemporary ecosystem. The challenging factors that come along with e-resources, such as multiple pricing models, publisher-specific licenses, various access options, and increasing preference for mobile devices is simply overwhelming. At the same time, this dynamic environment provides many new kinds of opportunities.

However, along with additional steps necessary to shepherd e-content through the acquisitions and access processes, technology may also provide some critical time-saving solutions. Options for electronically delivered invoices, the provision of machine-readable cataloging (MARC) record files, and customizable usage statistics may make the trade-off not only worthwhile, but even advantageous. Though it may not be possible to establish the same kind of regular workflow that could be achieved with an item-based acquisitions program, new technology-based services can allow acquisitions practitioners to recoup some of the time needed for acquiring e-resources. Knowing and leveraging the available service options from publishers and vendors is an important part of using time strategically.

For example, the time taken to negotiate and set up access to a large e-journal package might be somewhat offset in the long run by having publisher-supplied MARC records—if the records did not require significant editing in-house—and an automated usage statistics service that replaces an in-house system requiring manual tabulation. It is important to note, though, that any time saved may be on the institutional level and not necessarily in acquisitions. In fact, electronic resources may actually bring additional work to the acquisitions unit. Beyond ordering, establishing access, and paying for these resources, acquisitions personnel may be tasked with maintaining access and facilitating discovery for these resources on an ongoing basis.

One way of dealing with this destabilization in the information environment is to avoid overly rigid workflows, especially those based on assumptions of stability in the information environment. Processes in acquisitions have tended to be formulated in terms of linear and concrete steps presumed to encompass all the content that could potentially be added to a collection. However, such practices may not be effective when dealing with the constantly emerging challenges in the contemporary information environment. Formulating workflow in terms of the shared goals or ideals of the library, particularly concerning potential and intended access, acquisitions will operate with more flexibility, intention, and relevance. While predetermined workflows will still be required to process certain kinds of content in some cases, a successful acquisitions strategy will not be premised on the assumption that all content can be treated in a uniform manner. This is especially the case when an acquisitions program involves many formats (see discussion in chapter 3).

However, while many changes have impacted—and continue to impact—acquisitions, the core responsibilities, and therefore general competencies, have remained basically the same. An acquisitions professional's responsibilities will likely comprise an assemblage that includes several key, interrelated components:

- *verification* of the existence of selected content;
- *sourcing* of selected content (including format options, price, and availability);
- *ordering* with the most appropriate supplier;
- *encumbering* associated funds;
- *following* up on unfulfilled orders (including claiming or canceling orders);
- *receiving* physical materials;
- *establishing* access to online content;
- *paying* invoices and documenting payment; and
- *monitoring* the library's acquisitions budget.

Much of the fundamental confusion related to the complex nature of acquisitions originates with that initial misunderstanding of its basic role, stemming in part from the localized nature of the practices established to fulfill these responsibilities. Acquisitions, with its traditional focus almost entirely on the *item*, is a hybrid of library functions; being neither entirely process-based nor entirely content-based, acquisitions occupies a unique place within the library, which is further elaborated on in chapter 4.

The Information Ecosystem

Acquisitions is primarily concerned with *published* content requiring payment to obtain ownership or access rights. Publishing has many connotations, depending on context. In the following discussion, "to **publish**" means to formally prepare content and make it publicly available. In the context of acquisitions, publishing is typically done as a professional process—an assemblage that includes organizational components such as editing, compositing, and marketing. In other words, the majority of acquisitions work involves finished content.

Published content is sometimes free but most often acquired at a cost, either through purchase or lease (that is, limited-term acquisition). This content may be sold or licensed directly by the publisher or by a third-party entity. Such third parties (or **vendors**) are entities that resell, license, and/or aggregate already published content. Vendors typically make transactions easier by acting as a consolidated payment and service point for the publishers that they represent. Vendors are a business assemblage of published content.

A critical aspect of acquisitions is understanding how these entities interact in the information ecosystem. One longstanding assumption about the information ecosystem that must be reconsidered is the notion of the supply chains that operate within it. Supply of information to or within the library has traditionally been thought of in terms of linear models. Information flowing into the library has followed a fixed path of discovery and delivery. In such a model, the library is situated at the end of the chain—the information warehouse, which suggests that the role of the library in collecting—and therefore providing—information is consumer-based. It belies the library's necessarily complex role as a broker of scholarly communication and catalyst in the research process. The library's traditional internal supply chain can be thought of as a similar, even parallel static model resembling a chain. In this model, acquisitions has often ended up situated between the selection and access functions, creating a bridge between published content and information discovery by functioning as the mechanism "getting things." Such a static model represents an acquisitions process based on procurement, and may be reduced to the singular function of buying commodities. Significantly, this representational supply chain does not typically factor in the complex kinds of problem solving that any practitioner of contemporary acquisitions faces when expanding the library's assemblage of access.

These kind of models, which fix both acquisitions and the library in a static position in their respective information supply chains, are less relevant as the information ecosystem becomes more diverse and more complex. In the first model above, the library is positioned as an end point for the process of information dissemination, a sort of warehouse that information eventually trickles down to. This implies a somewhat passive role of the library within the broader ecosystem—collection of content as an end in itself. In the second model, acquisitions functions merely as an intermediary, positioned to react to order requests from collection development, then react again to the provision of content from the respective suppliers. These chains are part of a semantic geography of information based on a process of moving; they are fixed paths developed for transporting physical items.

The rigidity of such models is well suited to an older paradigm of information distribution, discovery, and access where linear movement of information could be safely assumed and access outcomes were fairly predictable. However, the nonlinearity of electronic resources is well established (Burnette, 2008), and this breakdown of traditional lines of acquisition has come to affect all possible formats (see chapter 3). In a very real sense, pathways of information creation, communication, and consumption form more than a simple chain: the pathways are mobile, asynchronous, decentralized, and hyperlinked. Just as other complex ecologies are recognized for their interconnectedness, relationships within the information ecosystem involve more than linear transmission.

In these models, acquisitions ends up situated between two intellectual processes. The first process involves the production of scholarly communication, where information is published as content. The second process is dissemination, of which collection-building is a part. Scholarly communication is selected, collected, and made accessible according to the mission and service goals of the library. This collection is built with the anticipation that it will hopefully be of use to the community it supports at some point. Acquisitions ends up having a kind of mediating role where its primary function is to be the bridge between two processes: one where content is identified and selected, and another where that content is made available to library users through a number of established channels.

When the supply of and demand for information were achieved through a model that assumed the primacy of paper, the notion of the supply chain and the accompanying (relatively) fixed channels of communication were fairly easy to understand. In all cases, there was something physical that had to be acted upon, something tangible: information could be shipped, stamped, shelved, and (possibly) circulated. To create efficiency in a process of moving things from multiple publishers to multiple libraries, the rise of third-party vendors (also called "**jobbers**" in the book trade and "**subscription agents**" in the serials business) was natural. The vendors became a single service point for libraries to work with and, in basic terms, continue to provide the same kinds of services at the present time for physical-format media. Jobbers, for example, allow for shipping, invoicing, and claiming from a single service point. Serials agents function slightly differently, handling renewals, invoicing, and claiming but not usually handling the actual physical issues in a subscription. The mediating role of vendors in terms of physical items is critical: by centralizing the functions associated with distribution, leveraging high-volume ordering per publisher to maximize discounts, and consolidating the service points for all publishers and libraries with whom the vendor does business, a maximum efficiency, and therefore savings, can be achieved.

Working with Vendors

Vendors are strategic partners in creating the assemblage of access through which the library connects to content of increasing amount and variety (see chapter 3). While their role in the emerging electronic information marketplace was once uncertain, the value that vendors add is evolving as the information ecosystem continues to change. While continuing to offer consolidated customer service and invoicing, most vendors have also developed sophisticated technology tools that can facilitate searching for and de-duplicating selected content, placing and managing orders, retrieving invoices, submitting payments, and—increasingly—providing various reports covering cost, usage, and subject matter. With the explosion of available and therefore potentially discoverable information, the library must continue to find ways to work through strategic partnerships to keep up with changes in content production and demand for various kinds of information.

Since most of the content that the library provides access to is published outside the library, work with vendors is a key role for acquisitions. Once establishing a partnership with a vendor (or several vendors), the role of acquisitions becomes slightly more complicated. Vendors simplify the acquisitions of material in many ways, but they also add value in many other ways as a service provider. When working with the vendor, available services become another mechanism through which content acquisition can be actively managed. In addition to supplying materials, a vendor also can consolidate information and streamline services that can be directly built into the library's assemblage of access. Vendor-supplied services might include:

- provision of prepublication data from multiple publishers;
- status change of publications;
- supply of content in a variety of media;
- discounts for volume purchasing;
- inventory of physical items or access models for e-content;
- full-text previews of e-resource content;
- Web-based selection, ordering, and invoicing tools;
- subscription renewal processing;
- bibliographic records (possibly with enhancements); and
- consolidated invoicing.

Often a vendor will provide value-added information and services online through mechanisms like Web interfaces, automated notifications (including "eSlips" for new books, frequency changes for serials, etc.), and **electronic data interchange (EDI)**. These online services were long ago recognized as necessary to simultaneously compensate for diminishing numbers of technical services staff while meeting user expectations of ever-faster content delivery times (Flowers and Perry, 2002). With the increasing expectation of real-time access to resources (or at least information about resources), a highly functional and flexible online presence is essential.

When it was limited to physical items that were created through a means of mechanical production (or reproduction) and physical distribution, the role of acquisitions was secured in a fixed chain that mediated selection of and access to content. In a sense, acquisitions practitioners were almost entirely concerned with getting a content container (e.g., a book) into the building—with the building itself functioning as a sort of "meta-container": a container that itself held more containers. This resulted in a linear model of collection building that was unidirectional and inflexible. However, when not completely tied to physical-format items, the linearity of the process breaks down. In collections that include intangible media, such as eBooks, e-journals, and streaming videos, the entire approach must change (see chapter 3).

Vendors tend to be thought of in fairly simple terms—for example, a means of obtaining discounting on content. Pricing is definitely part of the calculus used when selecting a vendor, consistent with the second principle of acquisitions practice, which affirms that an acquisitions librarian "strives to obtain the maximum ultimate value of each dollar of expenditure" (ALCTS, 1994). But while the discount may be one important aspect when considering the library's budget, unit price is, in the end, only part of the calculus—this is especially the case for serials, where it is usual for the library to be assessed an overall service charge for their mix of subscription titles rather than a price reduction. Acquisitions requires a financial strategy, and part of that strategy inevitably focuses on financial considerations. More is at stake than just the proverbial bottom line when considering the role of the vendor for content provision, however. While acquisitions is partly about managing business transactions and relationships, it also encompasses customer service, technical processing, and product support, too. In fact, many products and services provided by vendors may come at an additional cost to the library but provide something of great value to users that justifies the cost.

Managing the incoming content in a timely manner (regardless of format), updating the online records, and processing materials for return constitute just a few areas of concern for an acquisitions practitioner that might be aided by vendor services. Working with a vendor to develop **shelf-ready** processing for items, record downloads for purchased materials, and a protocol for handling the return of items—either duplicated or damaged—is a critical element in the partnership that acquisitions must forge with library vendors. By emphasizing the role of the vendor as an overall *strategic* partner rather than just a business partner, a given acquisitions operation is likely to achieve a great deal more than if the vendor is considered only in terms of the bottom line. Therefore, while considering the potential savings, the cost alone should not drive all acquisitions decisions. The second principle should be applied only in conjunction with the first, which "gives first consideration to the objectives and policies of his or her institution" (ALCTS, 1994). While financial considerations will be a part of an institution's objectives and policies, ultimately service will play a key role as well. Discussing the library's strategy with vendors and understanding, in turn, each vendor's available services and service limitations will allow acquisitions to support library end users according to the library's mission. And, of course, by striving to "remain alert to the underlying values and ethical issues in our transactions with one another and be as open and honest in our communications as possible . . . we can build long-lasting relationships of trust that will enable us to work together in ethical ways," allowing us to meet user needs and expectations (Flowers, 2002: 454).

SELECTING A VENDOR

Methods for selecting a vendor may include the following:

- formal request for proposal (RFP);
- professional references;
- vendor visit to campus;
- librarian, staff, and/or administrator visit to vendor site;
- conference presentations; and/or
- mandate from a procurement or administrative office.

Some considerations when making a vendor selection include:

- pricing of content (including discount structure and any service fees);
- shipping (costs, packing options, scheduling);
- Web-based account management system (including tracking orders and retrieving invoices);
- physical processing (if applicable) and associated costs;
- E-content licensing and registration (if applicable);
- approval plan (see below);
- availability of demand-driven book or pay-per-view article acquisition;
- return and cancellation policy (including credits);
- invoicing format and payment terms; and
- level of customer service.

Developing a significant role for a particular vendor within the acquisitions assemblage is important. Ultimately, all of vendors with whom the library partners should have a clearly identified role that adds value in some way to the acquisitions process and, ultimately, overall library service. Articulating this role must start before a vendor is selected, then reviewed and affirmed as long as the library works with that vendor. For example, acquisitions professionals, in conjunction with other stakeholders in the library, must be able to clearly define not only the pricing parameters for acquiring particular content, but also any additional value-added services that a vendor may also provide. Such services might include those that support the physical collection, such as **physical processing** of print books, including full preparation of shelf-ready materials. Or, in the case of electronic resources, the negotiation of boilerplate license terms for e-resources like journal packages or databases. Services might also include customization of the interface to the vendor's Web site or the format that the invoices are delivered in. Most vendors are fairly flexible in terms of what services they can provide and what options are available within those services. Frequently it comes down to how valuable any given service is to the library. Questions that guide a decision about using a particular vendor service include:

- Is this service something that the library needs?
- If the service is not necessary, does it significantly enhance access to or use of associated content?
- Can the service be provided by the current library staff?
- Can the vendor-provided service meet (or exceed) the library's quality standards?
- Is it more cost- and/or time-effective for the vendor to provide this service?
- Can the library afford any additional costs associated with the service?

VENDORS AS PARTNERS

Choosing a vendor and developing a working relationship with that vendor is a critical part of the acquisitions assemblage. The partnership with each vendor that the library uses is an important connection between content publication and subsequent content consumption by library users. While vendors are businesses that are trying to make money, the value they add to content acquisitions should exceed what their services cost each respective library.

Vendors can offer many services. At their most basic, they provide a single point for order submissions and any subsequent claims, consolidated invoicing for content and any associated services, and regular delivery of content. Additionally, vendors might provide additional services such as processing of physical-format items, provision of bibliographic records for acquired content, and out-of-print searching.

Because the ability of the vendor to provide content and related services has such an impact on the library, vendor decisions should be carefully considered. In some cases, either the vendor or the library (or both) might require a signed contract in place before the vendor begins supplying content or services for which the library will be billed. This might be standard practice or only apply to a certain volume of business or type of service. When in doubt, checking with the library administration or campus procurement office may be a good first step. Traditionally, one method of identifying and choosing a vendor is through a formal **request for proposal (RFP)** process where vendors interested in doing business with the library may be thoroughly evaluated.

However, it is unlikely that an RFP will be required for every acquisition situation. In some cases, such as private institutions where a competitive bid may not be required, a formal RFP is likely to be rare. Also, consolidations among publishers and vendors increase the likelihood that particular content or a particular service is only available from a single source. Even in those cases where a competitive bid is generally required, the library may be able to provide a **sole source justification** to acquire unique content or a custom service.

Whether or not a vendor is being reviewed through a formal competitive process, several factors should be considered before selecting a vendor to supply either content or service. Some questions to keep in mind are:

- What is it that I am trying to acquire? What vendors specialize in this kind of content?
- What value will this vendor add to the acquisitions process (e.g., increased efficiency, significant discounting, quality customer support, etc.)?
- Are there other vendors that specialize in providing this particular content and/or service?
- Does this vendor deal only (or at least primarily) with the library community?
- What experiences have my colleagues and/or other libraries had with this vendor? Do my colleagues have experience with other vendors providing this same function or set of functions?
- What are my expectations for content delivery, invoicing, or customer service, etc.? Have I communicated these expectations to the vendor and received adequate assurance that my expectations will be met?
- Is the vendor financially sound?

When working with a vendor, it is better to discuss expectations, establish service benchmarks, and ask questions up front. While a formal RFP may specify many of the performance and cost requirements, any business relationship should be based on a mutual understanding of the library's content and service needs, on the one hand, and the vendor's ability to meet those needs, on the other.

When searching for a vendor, particularly a principal vendor or one that the library will be doing a large volume of business with, all of the financial and service requirements should be carefully documented. In the cases where an RFP is not issued, terms of the agreement should still be carefully documented in a memorandum of understanding (MOU). Whether considering all potential vendors, a select few prescreened vendors, or just a single source, it is important to outline and contextualize the library's expectations in a formal document agreed on by all parties. Any interested vendors doing business with the library should clearly communicate the services they can provide, their associated costs, and any other terms, conditions, or additional services that may be applied. Though typically the library is empowered to identify potential vendors and have input in the selection process, all or part of it may be subject to regulations set by the library administration, university or municipal procurement policies, or even state law. Libraries involved with one or more consortium may need to take preexisting commitments into account when considering vendors. Regardless of how the terms of the relationship are documented, written details of the parties' agreement will serve as a useful reference into the future.

It is important to note that the RFP process is a serious one, and should be treated as such at all times. Anyone involved with reviewing the responses to an RFP is expected to act ethically. Besides showing professional courtesy and respect to those vendors who are competing for the library's business, the acquisitions practitioner has an opportunity to review detailed and potentially sensitive information about each of the bidding vendors. Handling of such details is codified in the "Statement on Principles and Standards of Acquisitions Practice" (see sidebar above), requiring that the acquisitions professional "grants all competing vendors equal consideration insofar as the established policies of his or her library permit, and regards each transaction on its own merits" (ALCTS, 1994, Statement 3). Additionally, as the RFP may contain highly specific offers, it is also essential to keep in mind that an acquisitions professional is bound to obtain consent prior to using "original ideas and designs devised by one vendor for competitive purchasing purposes" (ALCTS, 1994, Statement 6). In circumstances where local policy requires an RFP and/or multiple bids prior to selecting a vendor, but the product(s) or service(s) can only be provided by a single vendor, a sole-source justification (and perhaps extra documentation) is generally required in advance of a commitment being formalized.

RFPs can be time-consuming and somewhat tedious to draft but represent a key tool for developing an effective plan, in terms of both content and budget. The important thing to keep in mind is that RFPs are useful only when identical or interchangeable items and services can be supplied from multiple vendors. This makes RFPs especially useful in the print-based world, where vendors can supply, for example, the same book or journal. However, where a product or service is uniquely offered from a single vendor—in the case of many databases or publisher-specific packages, for example, a route of direct negotiation must be taken. In these cases, the library and vendor are usually working either with a license or sole-source documentation. Negotiations provide the library some potential for lowering price, customizing access, or allowing some technical manipulation of the product. Negotiation, however, does not represent a free-for-all. While an acquisitions professional should give "first consideration to the objectives and policies of his or her institution" (ALCTS, 1994, Statement 1), it is critical that one "avoids **sharp practice**" (ALCTS, 1994, Statement 9) in working with sellers in any context. Whether working with a vendor through an RFP, a publisher during a license negotiation, or a customer service representative over a single book, professional and personal ethics matter. As a matter of course, it is expected that an acquisitions professional "fosters and promotes fair, ethical, and legal trade practices" (ALCTS, 1994, Statement 8).

Vendors can streamline processes while enhancing library service. Acquisitions professionals frequently rely on vendors to provide an assemblage of important services, such as consolidated purchasing (including ordering, shipping, and invoicing), competitive pricing, and ultimately, value-added services that ultimately benefit users. Vendors are also a source for other kinds of valuable services, such as supplying information about forthcoming publications, troubleshooting technical difficulties, and structuring models of content acquisition that are customized for a particular library's situation. This means that the library's assemblage of access is highly dependent on relationships with the content and service providers that partner with acquisitions. While technology mediates many interactions between acquisitions and the vendors they work with — whether it be via telephone, fax, e-mail, or Web site — work with vendors is often conducted on a personal level. For librarians, having a designated contact in situations requiring a quick response can result in rapid and effective problem solving. For example, if a requested book arrives damaged, a popular database goes down, or a quote for a major reference product is needed before the end of a fiscal year, being able to reach out directly to a known individual on the vendor side can make a huge difference in terms of time and efficiency. Vendor representatives, on the other hand, look to personal contacts in libraries to reach out to regarding new or forthcoming products, provide feedback about existing products and services, and contact about licensing, among many other functions. The personal quality of these professional relationships ensures that ongoing interactions in a changing information ecosystem are relevant, impactful, and mutually beneficial.

In working with vendors and publishers, it is essential for acquisitions professionals to keep in mind at all times that business is — or potentially is — being conducted and that everyone involved should act accordingly. Even when interactions become friendly and informal, they should always remain ethical. Of course, being professional does not preclude either friendliness or informality — in those cases where informality is appropriate. Vendors still invest considerable resources (both time and money) in establishing and maintaining personal relationships with the libraries that they do — or might do — business with. The most obvious manifestation of that investment is sending out their representatives to meet with librarians and other interested parties in person. Often, such site visits or conference interactions might seem like nothing more than sales calls — and in some cases they might be just that — but such in-person meetings also provide a chance to interact with a colleague on a personal level. These visits should be viewed as opportunities to have the focused and undivided attention of a company's agent. To capitalize on such opportunities, a librarian "accords a prompt and courteous reception insofar as conditions permit to all who call on legitimate business missions" (ALCTS, 1994, Statement 7). These interactions can be an ideal situation to share with the vendor representative the library's service and content needs, provide a realistic outlook on resources, and explain the long-term strategic goals of the collection development strategy. Once trust and rapport have been established, site visits and any subsequent negotiations need not be a "black box" where intentions are not clear and goals are obscured — transparency will inevitably help both sides best reach their objectives. By communicating directly and honestly, librarians can then leverage the time that they have scheduled to work with a vendor to reach an outcome that is mutually beneficial. While this approach clearly applies to site visits from representatives, it applies as well to phone calls and even e-mail messages.

Since all relationships with vendors are predicated on the real or potential business that a library conducts with them, it is imperative that everyone involved "subscribes to and works for honesty, truth, and fairness in buying and selling, and denounces all forms and manifestations of bribery" (ALCTS, 1994, Statement 4). Decisions to work with particular vendors and publishers should be made objectively, to ensure that the fairest (though not necessarily cheapest) prices and best services are obtained on behalf of the library's users. In an effort to avoid any conflict of interest or favoritism, real or perceived, it is necessary that a librarian "declines personal gifts and gratuities" (ALCTS, 1994, Statement 5). As previously discussed, it is important that the process for selecting a vendor in a given situation is equitable so that any decision results in the best value for the library and library users. Evidence-based decisions should include written descriptions of both parties' expectations and obligations, a demonstration of the vendor's products and services, and a clear statement of the library's collection and access strategy.

Sometimes, a more informal approach is needed for singular, more unique content. In terms of speed and availability, the Web provides an enormous assemblage of content as well as, in many cases, multiple direct routes to that access. While this is obvious on one level, availability and speed are not the only variables that go into developing a successful Web-based acquisitions strategy. Like other aspects of contemporary library work, new challenges are frequently defined in terms of abundance rather than the scarcity that defined collection-building strategies of past ages. Like any kind of information search, knowing where and how to find the most relevant sources remains an essential skill.

Orders

Once a selection decision has been sent to acquisitions, the acquisitions process begins. As noted in chapter 1, ordering is one of the core competencies of acquisitions. There are three main kinds of orders: firm orders, standing orders, and subscriptions. These order types constitute the assemblage of ordering and correspond to different kinds of published content: **monographs**, (including **sets**), **series**, and **serials**. Order types are based on how the content is organized, not necessarily indicative of format.

Firm orders are those issued for a specific thing, such as a particular book. These orders represent a commitment by the library to buy, and therefore represent an assurance to the vendor that the thing will be paid for. A **standing order** is an open order for a series or **continuation**, representing an ongoing commitment to buy content as it is published. A standing order may be recurring (as in the case of annual publications) or open-ended. Series typically have a narrow focus and so do not represent a large commitment by the library; this is important given their uncertain publication schedule. (See chapter 4 for more about budgeting.) Finally, a **subscription** is a kind of order that commits the library to recurring payments for a given amount of time (usually a year) or a certain number parts (usually issues). Journals and newspapers are perhaps the best known, though libraries may also subscribe for other kinds of content, such as database access. In the case of electronic subscription content, a library may be acquiring **perpetual access** rights—that is, continued access even after a subscription is cancelled (this is sometimes a provision for e-journal subscriptions). But typically access is only granted for the duration of the subscription (a typical arrangement for databases). In cases where perpetual access to subscribed content is granted by the publisher or expected by the library, terms should be agreed to before the subscription starts and be clearly stated in the license.

The **approval plan** was developed as a method of bringing materials into the library's assemblage of access with a minimal amount of effort on the part of both the library and the book vendor. In fact, the approval plan functions as a component of the respective collection development and acquisitions assemblages. Through the approval plan, which today can function with a high degree of nuance and customization, content is both identified and delivered to the library automatically. With library-provided selection criteria, including subject (e.g., Library of Congress classification) and nonsubject criteria (e.g., publisher), monographs can easily be identified and provided by the vendor, maximizing the efficiency of the collection-building process. Such efficiency can be leveraged to help compensate for the number of available librarians (or amount of available librarian time) devoted to collection development; the approval plan can also secure access to new content far more quickly than traditional title-by-title selection.

Subject criteria are often based on either the Library of Congress or Dewey classification schemes. Those criteria considered "nonsubject" include categories such as publisher, series, or price limits. This allows maximum flexibility in designing a selection mechanism based on any number of pertinent factors as determined by the library. Many plans are sophisticated to the degree that as long as the library is able to provide a selection rule, the criteria can be used in defining the sphere of access made available by the vendor. Many approval plans include other optional services, such as enhanced catalog records for approval content, shelf-ready materials, or eBook provision, which are likewise part of the library's content profile.

Approval plans are offered by most major domestic and foreign vendors; configurations of the respective plans are specific to each vendor. It should be kept in mind that these plans, the instruments used to set them up, and the systems used to administer them are typically proprietary, incorporating "original ideas and designs devised by one vendor for competitive purchasing purposes" (ALCTS, 1994, Statement 6). Specifics from one vendor's plan should not be shared with another vendor.

At its core, the approval plan represents a kind of blurring of boundaries between collection development and acquisitions, as the plan automates several aspects of each respective function. As approval plans become more sophisticated, they likewise become more nuanced even as they become more totalizing; in other words, approval plans provide a means of applying increasingly granular selection rules to an increasingly large body of content. Despite the approval plan's fundamental grounding in the selection of content, management of the plan almost inevitably impacts acquisitions: ordering, shipping, invoicing, and returns all dovetail with the functioning of the plan. Therefore, it may make sense for the administration of the plan, typically via the vendor's online database, to be the responsibility of acquisitions. No matter who in the library is responsible for the maintenance of the library's plan, acquisitions must work closely with collection development in addition to the vendor.

A well-developed approval plan can draw a significant amount of content into the library's sphere. At its most basic level, the plan will provide an advanced notification system, either through the automatic supply of paper slips or, more frequently now, the provision of electronic title notification via eSlips according to the **profile**. The process of determining these criteria is an ongoing dialectic between the library and vendor that improves the accuracy and efficiency of the approval plan over time. The initial process of setting up a profile is intuitively called "profiling."

While many libraries have been reluctant to give up paper slips that traditional approval plans were originally built on, there are undeniable advantages to the use of electronic slips. Since the slips are really representative of the information in the vendor's database, eSlips can provide real-time updates on title availability, price, and order status, if the title was already acquired by the library. A vendor may also be able to load the library's holdings directly into their database, making that tool even more comprehensive. ESlips can also provide a strategic advantage in providing live links to reviews, tables of contents, and book jackets. Other advanced features may be available through eSlips, including subject and author information, links to other titles in a series, and shared information among other customers of that vendor. In some advanced systems, vendors may actually allow previews of eBook material, linked directly from the eSlip. In all, eSlips provide unprecedented access to content during the decision-making process.

With the highly flexible nature of most contemporary approval plans and numerous integrated service options available from vendors, libraries are able to partner with one or more vendors to create an expandable and customizable sphere of access. Those plans that capitalize on the online environment provide opportunities for discovery coupled with significant resources to aid in decision making. The Web-based vendor databases allow for streamlined selection, efficient ordering, and granular reporting, including some financial data. Since such nuanced and comprehensive systems encourage the consolidation of acquisitions functions, it is imperative that any vendor is carefully evaluated prior to establishing a business relationship. This can be achieved most successfully through a well-structured RFP that elicits a detailed response and encourages conversation. Discussion with colleagues, attendance at related conference sessions, and regular evaluation of the vendor can help ensure that quality is maintained on a continuous basis.

The result of developing an approval plan is a sophisticated tool for filtering and managing the ever-expanding information ecosystem while supporting a likewise ever-expanding array of library user needs and expectations. In addition to identifying mainstream publications from major publishers, a well-honed approval plan also has the potential to help bring **gray literature** into the library's sphere. Also called "fugitive literature" (Chapman, 2004: 30), this broad category of information includes many types of publications—including reports of all kinds, conference proceedings, technical papers, and other content that may be marginal in terms of established distribution channels. Besides limited distribution, a lack of indexing or other bibliographic control may also increase the difficulty of discovery (Plutchak, 2007). However, while difficult to identify, such content may nonetheless be essential to meeting user needs. Even when gray literature is covered by an approval plan, it is likely that some of this content will fall outside the approval profile and will need to be sought out directly by acquisitions, either through specialized vendors or even an open Web search. Additionally, gray literature might also fall into one of the categories of "free" content, discussed in chapter 3, and therefore not qualify for inclusion in an approval plan.

Another kind of profile-based acquisitions process, "patron-" or "demand-driven acquisitions" (DDA) will be described more in chapter 4.

APPROVAL PLANS

Approval plans represent a sophisticated, customizable tool that can be used to achieve the library's selection and acquisition goals with a minimum of effort and a maximum of efficiency. When implementing a new plan, modifying an existing plan, or changing approval vendors, the outcome of an approval plan depends on all stakeholders clearly articulating their goals for the plan at the outset and working collaboratively—both before and after the plan is in place—in order to develop and refine the plan over time.

EXAMPLE 1
Research Library

In the case of a large research library, the overall collection focus is likely to be on specialized collections carefully curated to meet the long-term needs of the research community. At the same time, the library will also support a large population of students and faculty who have need for a broad collection of general content for their studies and teaching. In this environment, it is often not feasible to pick general, mainstream titles individually. For the broad, basic coverage required by a large academic population, an approval plan can automate what would otherwise be a rote and time-consuming process through the selection and acquisition cycle. Besides having books selected and delivered automatically through an approval plan, the physical items can be processed by the vendor and come shelf-ready with customized physical processing, which might include bar codes, slip pockets, property stamps, radio-frequency identification (RFID) tags, call number labels, or security strips. Other processing options may be available, as well, though the amount of physical processing could significantly impact the per item price.

This level of automation allows the selectors to focus on their research areas, finding specialized content and investigating resources specific to their collections.

EXAMPLE 2
Liberal Arts College

Unlike a research university, most content acquired in a liberal arts college library may be focused on providing a wide variety of content for a primarily undergraduate population. Content supporting faculty teaching and research may also be in the mix, though likely a smaller part of the mix. Besides the difference in the size and needs of the library users, resources—including money, space, and personnel—are generally more limited than they are in a research environment. The library's content is more likely to support curricular and teaching needs rather than high-level research.

In this circumstance, the approval plan can be used in different ways than in a research library. One strategy might be to have most of the library's monographic content delivered on approval. Instead of relying on a book plan to fill in just the core of the collection, the process of building much of the collection can be mostly automated. This would relieve the librarians of almost all title-level collection decisions in order to focus on instruction and assisting students with individual research needs. Or the library could set up a slip-only plan. This would give the selectors more control over the budget, which can be critical in situations where the budget is small or funding is unstable. This option requires title-by-title decisions, though for a relatively small number of overall selections.

Because approval plans are adaptable, they can be customized to fit any situation. Besides the size and focus of a particular collection, plans can also be developed among two or more institutions to support collaborative collection development. However, because of the freedom in creating and administering an approval plan, it is important to always think about the library's mission and available resources when developing such a plan. Approval plans can also be integrated with demand-driven acquisitions (DDA) plans, described more in chapter 4.

BLANKET PLANS

Similar to approval plans are **blanket plans**. In these plans, libraries agree to accept and pay for all the content shipped by a vendor from a specific publisher or region. If effectively managed by both the vendor and the library, this can be a way to obtain difficult-to-find materials. Examples include all the content published by a given publisher, or all the available content published in a certain language in a particular country. Because the material provided on such a plan is both uncertain and nonreturnable, such a plan is best set up in support of an important research or teaching collection.

Strategic Assemblages of Access

The contemporary paradigm of acquisitions is most properly associated with access to content, rather than the purchase of materials. It is true librarianship consists of more than providing access to content; it is also true that other service areas of the library contribute to providing access to library users. However, libraries exist primarily to bring an assemblage of information in the form of content together in such a way as to make that content available and useful to users who need it. In other words, the core of the library is its collection. Access to that collection (or assemblage of collections) is a mission-driven function and a localized practice. Even the idea of what constitutes "access" becomes a context-specific concept. A library supporting a small liberal arts college may be most concerned with providing a breadth of content that is readily accessible. A library at a research university may be more focused on the future access of information, especially in particular subject areas, which results in an anticipated rather than an acute information need. A public library might be most concerned with practical and popular kinds of content that have broad appeal within the local user population. In all these cases, there are likely special collections that are unique and serve one or many different functions beyond the scope of the general collection. The changing and expanding information ecosystem does not undermine the need for unique content, locally focused collections, or long-term preservation as demanded by a given situation. However, changes in content production and consumption complicate both the mission and the practice of every library in terms of both access and preservation.

Access has become increasingly detached from ownership in many, though certainly not all, cases. This means that acquisitions may not always, or may not even mostly be dealing with straightforward purchasing of content. However, the proliferation of formats has also changed the nature of ownership. While ownership undoubtedly remains a requirement for certain kinds of content, a rigid dichotomy of "owning" or "not owning" is no longer the entirely meaningful principle that it once was. Lee (2000) has postulated moving away from such a dichotomy because of differences in the perceived meaning of the idea of ownership between information professionals and information users. While the latter focus on "access and convenience," the former "are mostly concerned with how to secure and control information resources as well as the legal ramifications of doing so" (Lee, 2000: 1108). The question of defining and managing ownership has become only more complicated as the Information Age matures. The result is an "ownership continuum," where the rights to access, archive, distribute, and so on for a particular content object can be thought of in terms of degrees instead of absolutes. For example, as noted above, subscriptions may include only temporary (subscribed) access, perpetual access to subscribed content, or a hybrid arrangement where some content is only available for the duration of the subscription while portions of the content may be available in perpetuity. This shift to a more nuanced approach to access rights has evolved in much the same way as the now-superseded dichotomy of "print vs. electronic," which is discussed in detail in chapter 3.

OWNERSHIP CONSIDERATIONS

In a print collection, ownership and perpetual access are implied in the acquisition (i.e., purchase) of content, even if that perpetual access is not guaranteed (e.g., items can be stolen, destroyed, etc.). With the ascendance of e-resources, perpetual access must be explicitly provided by the publisher and often must be specifically negotiated for by the library. The access requirements in any given acquisitions situation are likely to be variable and contingent on several factors, such as the library's mission, the materials budget, and even the specific resource being acquired.

1. **The mission:** Who is using the collection? Is library content supporting a general curriculum, an interdisciplinary project, or a comprehensive research collection? The resources being acquired will need to be managed in light of their intended or probable use starting at the beginning of the acquisitions process to ensure that those resources support the end users for whom the content is being acquired.

2. **The budget:** Options for access may, in the end, depend on the budget despite all other considerations. While perpetual access might be a stated ideal of a particular acquisitions program, it simply may not be possible. As budgets continue to tighten, a strategic balance between owning a limited amount of content in perpetuity and accessing a broader range of user-requested content in a timely manner will become more important even as it becomes more difficult to manage. (For more on budgets, see chapter 5.)

3. **The resources:** In the end, it may not be necessary—or even desirable—to own all resources that the library users want to access, even if the library is in the enviable position of being able to buy all selected content. For many continuing e-resources, it may be better in the long run to lease or subscribe content. If content is updated regularly, paying an annual or per-access fee might be more cost effective and prove easier to manage in the long run than a collection that has to be actively managed by library professionals.

Regardless of where on the continuum of ownership the library's access rights fall, the library will likely have to pay for those rights, whether access is through ownership, site license, or pay-per-view. This will include directly tracking the library's budget allocation(s) for content acquisition while staying aware of external economic conditions. Variables such as global financial crises, university budget projections, and currency exchange rates should be accounted for when monitoring the library's own funding. To maintain access, whether in the form of regularly scheduled book shipments or uninterrupted database searching, invoices should be paid promptly.

Discrepancies between expected content and delivered content, which will inevitably arise, need to be brought to the vendor's attention immediately. Situations will vary and it should not automatically be assumed that withholding the library's payment to a given vendor is the most appropriate way of dealing with problems or misunderstandings. Possible remedies for invoicing problems may include:

- returning wrong or damaged materials,
- crossing a line item off the invoice prior to payment,
- having a subscription extended, or
- receiving a credit memo from the vendor to indicate that a payment has been credited to the library's account.

Ethically, honest communication almost always trumps rash action. Communication to the vendor should be prompt and, where necessary, appropriately documented.

Many libraries do not directly pay vendors for content but rather have payment issued through a central payments office on campus or a municipal office. While more efficient and secure for the administrative entity, such a process often results in a lag between the processing of an invoice in acquisitions and payment being issued to vendors by the university. Most library vendors are set up to accommodate the delay. Several options may be considered for expediting payments when necessary, though all such options are subject to local contingencies and regulations. One option is connecting the acquisitions module of the ILS directly to the university accounting system to process payments directly in the library system. While this can be a very effective means of getting payments processed and issued to vendors, the technical barriers to such an interface can be substantial. Acquisitions can also configure

electronic data interchange (EDI) with vendors to receive invoices electronically directly in the ILS. Again, such an exchange is dependent on the technical ability of both the library and the vendor(s) to implement such a process with their respective systems. One of the most effective means for issuing payment to a supplier is the use of an institutional credit or purchasing card, often referred to as a "**p-card.**" While the p-card allows for instantaneous payment, someone will be required to keep the appropriate records for purchases made with the p-card and balance the monthly statement. Such responsibility usually resides in acquisitions. Like any credit card, purchases may carry some risk, either because the Web connection is not encrypted or the account information is not kept secure buy the seller. When a p-card is issued to acquisitions, it is important to keep the account information secure in the library and watch the statements carefully to ensure that the account has not been compromised when making purchases throughout the month.

Instead of operating solely within an aggregated collection of physical items where access is achieved through a number of labor-intensive (if ingenious) analog access apparatuses, the library community must now be concerned with a more complicated assemblage of access. This would be all information available to the library community, whether or not it is owned by or contained in the library. This partial dissolution of the library as an entirely (or even principally) physical collection necessarily includes access points well beyond the scope of acquisitions, such as one library community's access to other libraries' resources—or even the open Internet (e.g., Google, etc.). However, the implications of this dissolution of the *library-as-a-building* for the organization and practice of acquisitions remains profound. In essence, the contemporary library collection is expandable in infinite directions; in theory, today's library collection may even be considered infinitely expandable. (See chapter 3 for more about Discovery.) It seems that the limits on potentially available information recede further into the distance with each passing day. Exceptions do, and will continue to, exist in the trends that drive the dissolution of the library as warehouse. Such notable exceptions include rare, local, and ephemeral materials. However, even in these cases—the rare books and the archives—the ability to produce digital copies (or "simulacra") of these objects is dissolving even this final frontier of physicality. Not that the originals can be entirely ignored or replaced, but that in many cases access to the copy of an item serves much the same purpose as access to the original. The exceptions to this streamlined access by way of virtual proxy will continue to be an ever-diminishing point on the access horizon.

Today, we must be more consistent about thinking in terms of *assemblages* rather than *collections*—even if the former term is not likely to replace the latter in our general discourse. This is not to diminish the role of the collection in meeting information needs, but instead to turn the traditional approach to access on its proverbial head. Rather than taking a permanent collection to be the primary mode of access, it is, instead, part of the makeup of the larger assemblage of access. This represents the ongoing diversification of content within the ecosystem. Content now arrives in many formats (see chapter 3), and the format of choice, where there is one to be made, will depend on need and preferred mode of access. Use of content is now more user driven, and therefore acquisitions must necessarily become at once more flexible as it becomes more complex. Acquisitions must also engage with the collection-building process in a more collaborative way, working closely not just with publishers and content vendors, but with other service units within the library and even with users. Such engagement follows Pritchard's definition of the "deconstructed" library, where the library is framed in terms of a "suite of services designed to meet a range of needs" rather than "a single definition of a collection in a building, designed to work in one, linear way" (Pritchard, 2008: 222). This flexible and collaborative approach requires a kind of processual nimbleness coupled with an expertise on available content sources in order to respond as rapidly as possible. Increasingly, acquisitions may even be working with the library users themselves in an expanded capacity. Some examples of content diversification within the information ecosystem that has directly impacted contemporary acquisitions include digitization of **local content** or other **rare content**, the expansion of **consortia** and other alliance-based information access, and the **open access** movement.

Conclusion: Strategic Access

While the dominant ideas for strategic acquisition of content in a paradigm based on print resources relied almost entirely on cost-cutting solutions for physical items—shipping, processing, receiving—these are now just a few of the elements that must be considered in contemporary acquisitions.

And while tangible material will clearly play some role in most collections indefinitely, the time and energy available for this kind of content is increasingly marginalized. Experience with e-journals, for example, has definitely proven diminishing returns for the inputs—time, energy, and money—that go into traditional print-based journal management and processing in cases where electronic access is available for general research needs. What is presented to the acquisitions practitioner today is a vast array of potential sources and possibilities for content production and dissemination. To meet the requirements of complex collection development and the increasingly sophisticated demands of library users, the acquisitions practitioner must be prepared to bring a nuanced strategic approach to both sourcing and providing access to required content.

This validates neither the long-anticipated "end of print" nor the similarly extreme assertion that "format does not matter." These two clichés were born with the World Wide Web and have proven to be quite pervasive concerns in terms of scholarly, professional, and popular culture. The expectation seems to be that either all information will be electronic (produced in or converted to an electronic-based format) or that so much information will be digitized that it will not matter if something happens to exist in print as long as it can be accessed online. The fact is that in some ways, print actually matters more than it ever has. Manhoff (2006) makes the compelling case that limitations inherent to the production and distribution of information objects in specific formats, including both print and electronic, means these objects, even when the information itself is identical, cannot be treated as the identical objects. Electronic formats will have their own distinct features and limitations, as will their print counterparts—if such counterparts exist. While acquisitions has always responded to the decision-making of collection development by finding an item that contains the content being sought, there is an emerging role for acquisitions to help identify the *specific* format once the content decision has been made by collection development. This implies an interaction both within the library and with the selected content beyond the traditional role of acquisitions. By extension, acquisitions needs to be included and specifically engaged in the larger intellectual and service mission of the library.

For libraries to succeed, it is critical that those who are organizing and practicing acquisitions take a proactive, forward-thinking role in developing techniques that are general and adaptable enough that they can provide access to many formats without necessarily assuming one to be dominant. Though it may be possible and perhaps necessary to establish and maintain several sub-processes within acquisitions (Burnette, 2008), a context-specific approach that is goal oriented rather than process oriented will be most appropriate. While utilizing routines where necessary, an approach focused on access outcomes will be more likely to absorb the constant irregularities of content acquisitions.

Acquisitions is an assemblage of basic functional categories (ordering, receiving, access, and payment) that draw on associated competencies and practices, where practitioners operate within an ethical framework. At the same time, significant changes in both the library and larger information environment have fundamentally altered what it means to "do acquisitions." The move away from static supply chains and storage of information within information ecosystem has resulted in a nuanced matrix of information production, dissemination, and consumption. Within this paradigm, the central function of acquisitions as a profession of a ethically based and strategy-driven information practice has not changed, but rather shifted to be one that demands a more proactive, synthesizing practice. User preference in both searching and accessing information has demonstrated a clear "shift of interest to the piece rather than the container, the article rather than the journal, the definition rather than the dictionary" (Van Orsdel, 2007: 204). This clear shift has been accelerated by the adoption of mobile technology and the expectation for 24/7 access. The disaggregation of units of information from composite wholes extends beyond journals and databases to both reference resources and even general academic texts, as eBook platforms allow both full-text searches of monographic content and subsequent results ranking by chapter. (See chapter 3 for more about eBooks.) The increasingly granular specificity of information sought by library users has significant implications for acquisitions, as changes in user demands will drive changes in the resources that are acquired.

The key to adapting in this new information paradigm "is in reorienting our work to a much more refined definition of services, focusing on unique strengths, local needs, and multiple ways of delivering information" (Pritchard, 2008: 222). The emerging information matrix has resulted in the need for a more collaborative and synthetic role of acquisitions within the library due to a proliferation in modes of access, along with the associated contingencies around remote access and complicated acquisitions models. With a multiplicity of formats making up this matrix, it will be critical to move beyond rigid distinctions of "outmoded categories" (Plutchak, 2007: 82). Practice within the complex and diverse information ecosystem will depend on reconsidering the way that information is produced, distributed, used . . . and acquired.

REFERENCES

ALCTS. 1994. "Statement on Principles and Standards of Acquisitions Practice." Acquisitions Section Ethics Task Force. Available: www.ala.org/advocacy/proethics/explanatory/acquisitions (accessed October 15, 2009).

Burnette, Elizabeth S. 2008. "Budgeting and Acquisitions." In *Managing the Transition from Print to Electronic Journals and Resources: A Guide for Library and Information Professionals* (pp. 3–27), edited by Maria D. D. Collins and Patrick L. Carr. New York: Routledge.

Carr, Patrick L. 2008. "From Innovation to Transformation: A Review of the 2006–07 Serials Literature." *Library Resources and Technical Services* 53, no. 1: 3–14.

Chapman, Liz. 2004. *Managing Acquisitions in Library and Information Services*, rev. ed. London: Facet Publishing.

Flowers, Janet L. 2002. "Ethics Within the Serials Family." *Library Collections, Acquisitions, & Technical Services* 26: 449–456.

Flowers, Janet L. and Scott Perry. 2002. "Vendor-Assisted E-Selection and Online Ordering: Optimal Conditions." *Library Collections, Acquisitions, & Technical Services* 26: 395–407.

Lee, Hur-Li. 2000. "What Is a Collection?" *Journal of the American Society for Information Science* 52, no. 12: 1106–1113.

Manhoff, Marlene. 2006. "The Materiality of Digital Collections: Theoretical and Historical Perspectives." *portal: Libraries and the Academy* 6, no. 3: 311–325.

Plutchak, T. Scott. 2007. "What's a Serial When You're Running on Internet Time?" *The Serials Librarian* 52, no. 1/2: 79–90.

Pritchard, Sarah M. 2008. "Deconstructing the Library: Reconceptualizing Collections, Spaces and Services." *Journal of Library Administration* 48, no. 2: 219–233.

Propas, Sharon, and Vicky Reich. 1995. "Postmodern Acquisitions." *Library Acquisitions: Practice and Theory* 19, no. 1: 43–48.

Van Orsdel, Lee C. 2007. "The State of Scholarly Communication: An Environmental Scan of Emerging Issues, Pitfalls, and Possibilities." *The Serials Librarian* 52, no. 1/2: 191–209.

CHAPTER **THREE**

Assemblages of Discovery

"Discovery" simply means "finding something," and usually conveys a sense of finding something *unexpected*. But discovery might entail something more than mere serendipity: it might require planning, decision making, even a journey. For our purposes, the assemblage of "discovery" will constitute a technologically mediated information context where content is found both intentionally and serendipitously (that is, by happy accident). To a degree, discovery has always been a recognized and important—perhaps even primary— function of libraries. Card catalogs, indexes, and classification systems made it possible to find both known and unknown information related to a topic or idea. This process of discovery was automated and expanded with the electronic card catalog and online indexes. However, leveraging the power of online search engines with the ever-expanding electronic content has expanded the reach, increased the accuracy, and improved the sophistication of library-mediated discovery.

DISCOVERY SERVICES

- EBSCO Discovery Service (EDS)
- Primo Central by Ex Libris (a ProQuest Company)
- Summon by ProQuest
- WorldCat Discovery by OCLC

Discovery

Along with an expanded understanding of the information ecosystem must come a fuller explanation regarding the nature of discovery by the end users who ultimately make use of library content. With the rise of **"Web-scale" discovery services** developed specifically for libraries, collections are at once more integrated and more fluid. A nuanced *understanding of* and *interaction with* content is required for acquisitions professionals striving to support the evolving library, and to keep practices moving forward into the future.

An investigation into discovery requires a detailed discussion of the concept of "format" and the implications it has for the creation, discovery, and dissemination of content. The transition to a discovery system requires what Howard and Wiebrands describe as a "radical shift in mindset" (2011: [10]). Within this shift,

> it is undeniable that our emerging concept (or concepts) of discovery are becoming more complex and nuanced as the information landscape becomes more difficult and confusing to navigate. The very idea of discovery is becoming inextricably tied to the library. And though this idea certainly carries the connotations of technological development and expanding access to content, it also provides a new framework in which to refine (or redefine) library collection and service models (Holden, 2013: 14).

The linear-chain models of workflow described in the previous chapter are premised on two other assumptions regarding acquisitions' role in the provision of content, neither of which should be taken for granted any longer. The first assumption is that acquisitions will primarily be purchasing physical materials to add to the library's tangible collection. The outcome of this assumption is the construction of a workflow around the addition of physical items to a permanent collection. The physical item, therefore, becomes the driver of the process.

The second assumption is that acquisitions is exclusively a component of the "technical services" assemblage (which, besides "acquisitions," encompasses other technically based assemblages, such as "metadata" and "systems"). It often follows from this assumption that acquisitions professionals are therefore separate from the "public service" assemblage within the library. The public service assemblage is comprised of the technologies and services with which library users typically interact, and is itself composed of smaller assemblages, such as the circulation assemblage and reference assemblage. However, with integrated discovery technologies and services, acquisitions may *also* be included within the public services assemblage.

The assumption that because acquisitions is generally a key assemblage within technical services (and not perceived to be a part of more public-facing services) results in both a theoretical and practical exclusion of acquisitions units from an active role in the greater service mission of the whole library. The end result of this line of thinking isolates acquisitions in a single, fixed position within the library assemblage, where it becomes practically synonymous with "procurement." Further, such a fixed position threatens to keep acquisitions isolated *from within* the overall functioning of the library. Yet, acquisitions is (and always has been) a key component of the discovery assemblage within the library and frequently interacts with library users in important ways.

Content Objects

To produce consistent, predictable, and reliable results, library acquisitions must be grounded in *what* is acted upon rather than *how* it is acted upon. What does that distinction mean? Before making a decision about an acquisition, one must take into account *what* is being acquired. Certainly libraries will continue to buy books. However, since most libraries will not acquire *only* books, and not only *print* books, an approach is needed that does not start with thinking in terms of an item (e.g., "a book") but rather in terms of a format (e.g., "an eBook"). Why is this subtle difference important? The key is that digital production, reproduction, delivery, and access have changed the rules quite a bit from the days when "a book was a book." *Conceptions of* and *practices with* information (and content, specifically) continue to change expectations of what roles both the library and end user play in the ecosystem.

Following Manhoff's (2006) investigation of the materiality of digital objects, it is useful to revisit the idea of the *item* in the context of the library assemblage (and, subsequently, within the collection assemblage, etc.) and its impact on access and the acquisitions process within that assemblage. The **format**, as the technological means used both to inscribe, transmit, and read (in the broadest possible sense) particular content, exists as an **object**: that is, the content exists as something *material* but not necessarily *physical*. A "collection assemblage" needs to be approached not as items organized by formats but rather as formats embodied within particular objects—objects which may or may not be physical entities.

The implication that follows is *not* that we have moved somehow into a "post-format" environment where content is freed from its matrix of inscription. Though stressing the importance of *"the work"* (as an object) over *the document* (as an item) is not an entirely new approach (Smiraglia, 2003), our emerging understanding of discovery has facilitated a shift from a vague *association* of format and description with a particular work to a more precise *practice* of format that capitalizes on the nuances of inscription and, increasingly, metadata that are inherent to given information objects. This is primarily driven by developments in the digital realm, of course, but does not suggest a hierarchy assuming *superiority of* or even *preference for* digital formats. Instead, we have a situation where the implications of an information object's materiality (in contrast to physicality) means something substantially more than that it simply exists in a fixed place in the ecosystem. Now, rather than *items*, the object of acquisitions is quite literally the *object*—the intersection of content, format, and access.

Increasingly, discovery ensures that access may be ultimately established to a multiplicity of formats. This includes traditional print books and periodicals, of course, but may include other available formats that are more appropriate for a given use. Such formats may include electronic books (perhaps running on multiple platforms and available on a variety of devices), e-journals, databases, and disc-based or streaming media. If we were to consider an acquisitions assemblage in terms of formats instead of items, what would it consist of?

If *items* are individual physical things, then content must be abstracted to *objects* so that workflows can be structured in terms of the *format* of content objects rather than items. This is an essential step in leveraging discovery services for acquisitions practice; the role of contemporary acquisitions is to connect with content no matter what its form, rather than merely "buying an item." This approach challenges some basic tenets that have grounded past acquisitions practices, especially the centrality of the book as it has traditionally been understood. This shift positions acquisitions practice beyond the notion that "a book is just a book," and establishes the *process of discovery* as an intrinsic element of acquisitions practice rather than the more familiar and direct (and typically less complicated) *act of purchasing.*

Even the print-based approach is not as straightforward as it first appears. Printed content does provide a number of options for acquisitions, which requires a certain kind of strategic approach of its own. Of course, the options for print formats are inevitably item-based, given their inherent physicality. Therefore, actions that may be performed *on* or *with* a physical item are constrained by space and time. With print objects, one is presented with a number of circumstances that can be thought of as "**contingencies.**" These contingencies are considerations that relate to the particular materiality of content objects. For example, contingencies might include the availability of a print book (such as "in stock," "out of print," etc.), a particular print book's condition (such as "new," "used," "damaged," etc.), or any other factor that may affect its availability, usability, and value.

Likewise, contingencies exist for electronic content as well, but of an entirely different nature. *Access to* and *use of* e-objects can be affected, for example, by how the library pays for the content. E-Journal and database subscriptions often have an explicit duration (and sometimes an implied impermanence or instability) and may have certain uses curtailed by a license or embedded software. Electronic objects may appear or function differently depending on how they are accessed, such as through a desktop computer versus a mobile device. It is the growing number of format options and content configurations—especially in the push for online access—that has broken down the relatively rigid and stable structures that have previously made it possible to develop highly efficient workflow in both publishing (production and distribution) and libraries (collection development and management). Simultaneously, however, these same available options and configurations have provided an incredible amount of opportunity for discovery, and subsequent flexibility within acquisitions practice.

Interestingly, this approach starts to blur some traditional lines of how content is handled by the library. As acquisitions acts to build an assemblage of content in the present information ecosystem, then the familiar notion of the physical collection no longer adequately frames the concept of acquisitions. This shift even calls into question other traditional divisions within the library, such as interlibrary loan (ILL) and document delivery—which are often considered discrete and specialized functions completely separate from "acquisitions." While these arrangements may seem natural in some organizations, increasingly integrated and complex discovery services make possible a more holistic assemblage of content acquisition where these distinctions may not be as clear or as important. It may be that in the process of increasing flexibility to meet contemporary user needs that both ILL and document delivery become partially (or even entirely) incorporated into the acquisitions assemblage.

eBooks as Assemblages

Going into any acquisitions situation, practitioners will always have two options: attempting to force content into fixed, item-based workflows or developing a flexible, adaptive strategy that allows content to be acquired in virtually any format. Unfortunately, the tendency is to approach acquisitions with a set of established workflows and attempt to make everything fit into it. In a way, this makes sense: the more standardized the objects, then the more standardized the processes. In turn, standard processes allow the construction of efficient and predictable workflows. However, many content objects acquired by libraries cannot be standardized, for a variety of reasons. While it is not possible to enumerate all the contingencies (see above) that may complicate the acquisitions process, a strategic approach can be sketched by way of example. Perhaps the prime example of the possibilities and complexities inherent in acquisitions is eBooks.

Even within broad traditional categories of content (monographs, journals, etc.), formats can vary quite a bit. These broad categories are analogous to how content is treated within the catalog: They reflect the *form* of the content rather than the format. In determining workflows, an electronic book, or **eBook**, has the form of a monograph—in fact, the content and text is frequently identical to a print version (e.g., PDF). When working with eBooks, as with any format, trade-offs must be made. Physical books are a proven technology that both library staff and users are generally familiar with: they are known to be durable, do not require electronic mediation to access the content, and their tangibility is comfortable to many users. eBooks, on the other hand, provide speed of delivery, ease of access (including full-text searching), streamlined processing, as well as portability and saving of shelf space. eBooks have the possibility to provide enhanced navigation (hyperlinked navigation, such as table of contents and foot/endnotes), though they do not always take full advantage of this kind of enhancement.

Print books offer relatively few options, given that their format is fixed, with the attendant contingencies of having a physical manifestation. Pricing is per item (that is, volume or set), access is based on physical storage and delivery, and, being printed on paper, the text size and font is fixed. Inventory of physical items requires special identification (e.g., classification number and label) and tracking system (ILS or card file).

In contrast to the more traditional print book, eBooks offer a more versatile array of acquisitions possibilities. The pricing, access, and dis-covery assemblage(s) for eBooks is far more flexible, and various options favored by publishers, libraries, and users push development of both tech-nologies and policies in several directions simultaneously. Users may real-ize a number of functional advantages with eBooks, including enhanced discovery, simultaneous access for multiple users, off-site access, down-loading to personal electronic devices, and integrated tools like book-marking and note-taking. Though the various publication, access, and pricing models for eBooks are trending towards stabilization, this format still creates challenges in the acquisitions process.

eBooks 1: A La Carte

For the most part, we equate an "eBook" with an electronic monograph. Consumer eBooks have been made familiar to the general public through Amazon's Kindle and Apple's iBooks, which provide sales of eBooks from numerous publishers directly to individual consumers. Purchases from large, consumer-oriented online retailers like Amazon or iTunes are usually restricted for sale to individuals with no real provision for the kind of collective (and perhaps archival or even transformational) use of a work that is expected in a library context. Therefore, the library market is supplied with eBooks through two major assemblages: directly through publishers (especially in the Science/Technology/Engineering/Medicine, or STEM market) and through third-party vendors or aggregators. Like print books, eBooks can generally be purchased on a title-by-title or "a la carte" basis. This allows some integration with both established selection and acquisition workflows.

Aggregators are entities that provide access to books originally published by another entity but, in essence, re-publish the digital edition on a proprietary **platform**. The platform is the technology through which the user accesses and navigates content, and is usually equated by the end user with the online interface. Today, most platforms are Web-based and hosted remotely "in the cloud" (rather than on-site by the library). Now eBooks are firmly integrated into general acquisitions workflows, and can usually be included in firm order and approval plan workflows alongside print monographs.

Examples of eBook **Publishers**

■ Elsevier ■ SpringerTaylor & Francis ■ Wiley

Examples of eBook **Aggregators**

■ Books at JSTOR
■ EBSCO eBooks
■ Kindle (Amazon)
■ MyiLibrary (Ingram)

■ OverDrive
■ Project MUSE
■ ProQuest Ebook Central
(formerly EBL and ebrary)

---

eBooks 2: Bundles

While print books can be bundled for sale or lease in various ways, options for the acquisition of eBook bundles tend to be more numerous and varied. In fact, acquiring a group of eBooks might seem more like buying (or building) a database than purchasing a grouping of print books. This is one place where a traditional approach to—and assumptions about—acquisitions could hamper the process. As mentioned above, the title-by-title ("a la carte" selection-to-acquisition process is an extension of the traditional print model; eBook and print workflows are becoming increasingly and more seamlessly integrated. But the variety of eBook bundling provides myriad options for pricing, access, and grouping that is not possible (or at least not available) with print books.

The contingencies that come into play for bundled eBooks include the availability of instant (or near-instant) access for multiple users, the option to provide this access through a unified platform (and the corresponding ability to search through many or all books simultaneously), and the ability to add or remove titles from a given platform seamlessly.

One way to bundle eBooks is through package purchases. These sets are defined by certain subject and/or publisher parameters that usually allow a critical mass of titles to be bought in perpetuity at a favorable price. Packages may be groups of titles assembled by the publisher, sets of titles on a particular subject put together by aggregators, or a custom arrangement provide through a **consortial** agreement. Most of these packages contain a fixed number of titles selected by the vendor, aggregator, or **consortium**; therefore, the library may trade granularity of selection for advantageous pricing or time-saving decision making. Like a la carte selections, purchased titles are usually hosted by the publisher and likewise made available through a proprietary platform.

Collections of eBooks may also be offered on a subscription basis. Like perpetual access packages, subscription collections can be based on subject, publisher, and/or currency (e.g., front- or backlist). Since the library does not own these titles, access is all-or-nothing and limited to a paid period of time. Like most subscriptions, subscription periods are usually a year but might be two or more depending on the terms of the **license**. Content is accessed through the content provider's platform and so subscribed content may appear alongside (and, to the library user, indistinguishable from) "**perpetual access**" acquisitions. Significantly, the content of subscription packages may vary over time—even in the midst of a subscription term.

eBooks 3: Plans

One way the libraries save time, expedite access, and improve discovery (and ultimately use) of eBooks is by establishing content selection and acquisitions plans with vendors. eBooks from one or more publishers can be included in various collection-building plans, such as approval plans (described in chapter 2) or demand-driven acquisitions (DDA) plans (detailed in chapter 4). By leveraging traditional approval plans to incorporate eBooks, for example, eBook purchasing and access can be expedited. This approach can be utilized whether the plan is for eBooks only, "e-preferred" (where electronic format is given preference), or even if eBooks are just supplementing a primarily print-preferred plan.

Studies like the one conducted by Pickett, Tabacaru, and Harrell (2014) show how integration of eBooks into approval plans—especially the e-Preferred variety—can be employed as a valuable strategy for monograph acquisitions. In managing budgetary and staff constraints, a sophisticated understanding of these specialized acquisitions assemblages can be a critical tool.

With the ability to incorporate eBooks into many processes, the library can build an acquisition assemblage adaptable to many situations. Access may be further enhanced in several ways. As with traditional books, a bibliographic record can be added to the library catalog. Unlike the traditional means of access, however, an embedded hyperlink can connect would-be readers directly to eBooks. Users may access content directly through the eBook platform, either directly or by way of linking to a title through the catalog. The interface allows available eBooks to be searched like a database—searches may be either full-text or limited to the metadata provided by the vendor. Significantly, eBook content and metadata can also be integrated and searched through a discovery service. This allows books—even book chapters—to be searched, displayed, and accessed along with other content objects in the library's assemblage of access. This creates a seamless, if complex, way for researchers to access digital content from many publishers via many routes.

For the libraries, eBooks are an exemplar of the promise and practicality of an enriched information ecosystem. While not universally welcomed or accepted by users (Pyle, 2009), the ability to search and access books from virtually anywhere should have a profound impact on the way that content can be discovered and subsequently used. But as with any format options, there are trade-offs. Typically, printing and copying of eBook text is restricted to some degree by embedded **digital rights management** (DRM) in order to prevent unchecked reproduction and transmission of the content. Further, eBook formats are not necessarily conducive to every kind of use, either. Doctorow (2008) notes that because of the propensity to multitask within the networked environment, eBooks may not be well suited for reading long narratives (i.e., novels) on a computer or phone screen. Though much of the resistance preventing a wider acceptance of eBooks has been precisely the challenge of reading a long-format narrative, the constant improvement of eBook technology — particularly screen resolution — is changing that attitude in the consumer market. Significantly for libraries, as with any emerging electronic technology, there is some question about the long-term stability of the content. Even with the purchase of "perpetual access" titles (see above), how would the content be made available without the interface provided by the publisher? However, while reliable access to eBooks remains contingent on a number of factors, so, too, does reliable access to print books.

Emerging out of an intersection of a bulk, one-size-fits-all package purchase and highly-nuanced DDA plan — where usage determines what is purchased — is the "Evidence-Based Acquisitions" (EBA) model (Zhang, 2014). The EBA model employs usage data to maximize a libraries investment in high-use monograph acquisitions within a pre-defined budget from a single publisher:

> The idea behind EBA is that libraries pay an up-front fee for a particular collection that interests them. The content is then made available and usage recorded via COUNTER statistics. After six months or a year the [library or] consortium then buys books, based on use, up to the value of the up-front fee. Behind the basic business model there is a whole raft of considerations relating to content availability, discoverability, access and ownership (Alderson, 2014).

EBA therefore provides a means of broadening access to specific publisher's eBooks beyond the acquisitions budget in the short term while ensuring that the highest-used titles are held in perpetuity. Though not as sophisticated as a fully profiled DDA plan, EBA does provide some much needed flexibility as library budgets continue to shrink compared to the cost of available online content.

Online Ordering

For an individual consumer, retail and auction sites on the Web may seem more or less interchangeable. When making library acquisitions, it is important to remember that not all Web retailers and auction sites are the same. The differences, though, may not be immediately apparent. These differences can be subtle, but should be thoroughly investigated before making any kind of Web site a regular source for content acquisition. Though a Web retailer may be selected because of a unique product offering, a choice may be driven, consciously or not, because of perceived convenience or familiarity rather than true appropriateness of the retailer for content acquisition. Like other acquisitions decisions, neither brand strength nor personal familiarity alone should predetermine a decision about a content supplier.

Prior to making any kind of acquisition through a Web retailer, the content need as identified by collection development should be assessed to ensure that the combination of content and service is best met with a direct route to access. Often, services that are marketed by the online retailer may also be provided by one of the library's established vendors. Any time necessary access can be brokered through an established library vendor, that route should be given serious consideration because of the potential to save not only money but also time. With the proliferation of format options and limited staff time, it is essential that acquisition and access be made as efficient and reliable as possible. Working with a formal (or "traditional") library vendor allows for numerous advantages, which may include the potential for consolidated or electronic invoicing, substantial discounting, Web-based content management systems, or reduced shipping costs. Vendors may offer sophisticated inventory tracking through their online ordering interfaces, the same as many popular Web retailers, as well as the ability to work with publishers to **drop ship** items that are not stocked by the vendor.

If contingency makes the use of a Web retailer essential for providing access to content, it is important to know and understand the options that are available. The foremost consideration is that buying as an institution differs markedly from buying as an individual. The most important factor is whether a particular kind of acquisition is allowed by university or library policy. Some organizations, for example, may not permit purchases through an online auction site. If a staff member is using a Web site for library purchasing that might also be used for personal purchasing, separate accounts for library orders and payments will make library acquisitions easier to track. This separation can also prevent confusion later and possibly violations of institutional policy. Though it may seem obvious, it is imperative to keep personal shopping completely separate from institutional purchasing to avoid inadvertently paying for personal items with library funds.

While not all Web retailers require a credit card, almost all such sites accept credit card payments. Again, the rules regulating credit card use vary significantly depending on the library or perhaps even the specific situation within a given library. Because of the inherent risk in using a credit card in the online environment, it is critical that purchasing rules are completely understood prior to making any kind of credit card payment. Such understanding does not necessarily diminish the institutional risk that goes along with using a credit card, but can minimize personal liability if a card number is compromised. As with personal purchases, ensuring that a particular Web retailer is a reliable and trustworthy source makes good sense. For sites that are unfamiliar, checking with colleagues or requesting references via e-mail lists may provide some additional insight for doing business with such entities. Verifying that a site is secure (i.e., using encrypted transmission of sensitive data), usually identifiable by URLs prefaced with https://, is another precaution that may be taken prior to transmitting credit card information. Smaller independent or foreign sites may require the use of services such as PayPal to ensure secure financial transactions. Documentation for credit card transactions is important, both for future reference and for audit situations. A copy of the Web receipt should be saved, if possible, and it may also make sense to include any other supporting documentation (e.g., a copy of the order request from the selector) that the online site mails or e-mails. Local requirements for tracking and approving such transactions should be understood ahead of making any kind of credit card expenditure.

Some larger retailers, especially those that routinely work with libraries in some capacity, may offer invoicing options that do not require the use of a credit card. Setting up an account with an alternative payment option may provide an opportunity to streamline acquisitions made from that site. However, not all of these arrangements are ultimately advantageous for the library. Just as for a library vendor, no payment plan should be established or used without making careful consideration about the long-term ramifications of such a decision. Thought should be given to aspects of the retailer's service that could, in turn, impact the library's service. Awareness of how content will be paid for is critical. The option to pay an invoice rather than paying from a monthly credit statement can make payments easier to process, and more frequent payments will ensure that library **encumbrances** are up to date. The ability to directly contact a representative at the retailer, by either phone or e-mail, for problem solving and having the opportunity to establish a relationship with service representatives at the company will make the inevitable problems easier to solve. Many sites provide interfaces that are relatively easy to use; however, when making multiple purchases on an ongoing basis, the feedback and service mechanisms that underlie the technical aspects of the Web site are the keys to working with a retailer that will be supportive of acquisitions' role in the library. It is important to establish a service contact before a problem arises to ensure that a solution can be worked out expediently when necessary.

When purchasing direct from Web sites, familiarity and habit can lead to oversight. Even minor mistakes will end up being costly for the library—whether in time, money, or both. When using online retailers for acquisitions, perceived convenience must be tempered with full consideration of the high transaction cost of keying in order information, paying the shipping and handling on single items, and documenting credit card expenditures. Processing orders one title at a time loses any economy of scale; the redundancy in data entry, shipping charges, and handling costs may add to actual cost of the order as well as the opportunity costs in the additional time needed for library staff to process such orders. However, direct purchases from Web sites can significantly broaden the content available to the library and supplement vendor services in important ways.

FORMAT OPTIONS

If a library lost its copy of the book *Writing and Difference* by Jacques Derrida, for example, and the philosophy selector made the decision to replace it, this would initiate a series of decisions. The selector may indicate that a hard-copy replacement is required, though it is simultaneously available as an eBook. This is the most basic function in acquisitions: buying an in-print book from a major academic publisher.

This is an example of a monograph purchase. Though there are other kinds of formats that could be described as "monographic" (or singular, see definition above), a book is the exemplar of this category. Providing access to a monograph by way of adding printed books to the collection is what libraries have done most visibly, and the results generally meet library users' conditioned expectations. Additionally, since books have been a basically stable technology in terms of preservation and access, even legacy processes for acquiring books are generally adequate.

Frequently, a contemporary academic library cannot fulfill its function simply by adding books to the shelves. Though having a collection of books that meets users' needs and expectations is critical when such a format is required and available, it is only one part of the mission—and usually the easiest part. For a library to succeed, all units within the organization must be ready and willing to adapt to the expectations of their user community.

To be adaptable, flexibility is key. Keeping the example of eBooks in mind will be helpful (see above). In a situation where a user is concerned primarily about the content, acquisitions can be less focused on the item. In the instance where it is not required that a *physical* book be added to the collection, it may be that a selector provides instructions to get the content in any format. It is in cases like these that shifting from an *item*-based workflow to an *object*-centered one may useful. Or, it may be the case that a print book is needed but the desired time frame is flexible. When a request is not urgent, then the book can be acquired from the most appropriate source; "appropriate" may be determined according to price of the book, efficiency of acquiring it, payment method, etc.

Now, one can start to think strategically about what to do next.

At this point, there may be several options because the imperative is no longer just to "buy a book" but to get certain content according to particular parameters. Strategically, the *content object* may exist beyond the confines of a physical collection or may be available from several providers. Or perhaps the content is not even to be added to the collection at all, as is the case with ILL or document delivery. The goal now is to bring certain content into the library's collection assemblage, which may include used books or even eBooks. End use of material is a consideration not just for collection development professionals but frequently for acquisitions professionals, as well.

Conclusion: Ensuring Connectivity

One of the only ways to overcome the proliferation of formats, access models, and user preferences is to build versatility into the acquisitions process. This can be accomplished by cross-training staff and structuring the ordering process as efficiently as possible. Maintaining a variety of work flows is necessary to a degree, but steps should be standardized where possible. Also, establishing and maintaining effective, professional relationships with vendors will help ensure that the overall effectiveness of the acquisitions assemblage is maximized.

It is critical that collection building in libraries moves away from overly simplistic dichotomies such as print-or-electronic and ownership-or-access. Polarities such as these were useful for structuring discussions around the early Internet or nascent digitization technologies. However, with the maturing of the Web and the evolving best practices for digital content creation and conversion, the responsibility of ensuring access is best met with an array of options rather than a fixed course of action—especially when the surest way of ensuring access is traditional print materials. One way of meeting this challenge is by reevaluating the notion of format and its implications within the matrix of content production and communication.

Versatility will depend on the use of technology as an adaptable tool rather than an absolute limit. And technology will need to be employed creatively at all stages of scholarly communication. The further development of today's eBook platforms into multimedia content solutions will move acquisitions away from a strict focus on tangible-format media and allow for more accessible, flexible modes of access to non-print, non-textual information objects. However, print and other tangible media will continue to play a key role in the assurance of library user connectivity to content—both in the present and into the future. Publisher use of advanced print-on-demand technology has the potential to essentially end the notion of items being out of print, allowing text in digital format to be converted into print and acquired through established vendors whenever needed (Thatcher, 2009). Inclusion of such an option allows continuity of print in an increasingly electronic-based ecosystem. Finally, acquisitions must be prepared to adapt available technology to solve some of the puzzles created in the new information universe. For example, it may be possible to track electronic standing orders by creatively adapting publisher feeds rather than tracking new releases manually (for example, see Arch, 2009). Such automated notification to acquisitions can help staff manage content when items are not physically delivered to the library, and can therefore trigger the start of a "receipt" process that might otherwise be missed. Delivery of other kinds of data such as MARC records or **EDI** files can facilitate management, discovery, and access of acquired resources. For libraries, data transmissions from publishers and vendors provide the possibility of streamlining the acquisition and licensing of content through the use of an electronic resource management system (ERMS, discussed in chapter 4) or integration through the ILS. Such automation ensures options that allow for decisions to be made based on—rather than limited by—available formats.

Acquisitions plays a keystone role in connecting people with content. While this has always been the case, in the past, ensuring connectivity could have been equated with locating, ordering, and paying for physical items. Increasingly, the role that acquisitions plays in ensuring access takes on many forms and must be done at a higher level. Often, this higher level of access is mediated through a discovery service. Managing Web-based purchasing, profile-based plans, and novel access models are just some of the complex competencies that acquisitions professionals must manage. While a growing number of electronic formats has increased the available options for providing access, content inscribed within tangible formats (e.g., print books) remains an important part of developing the library's complete acquisitions assemblage. As more formats with different ordering, access, and maintenance requirements emerge and become discoverable, acquisitions work will inevitably only become more nuanced and complex. However, these often disparate-seeming tasks that typically fall to acquisitions can likewise be fitted systematically into a broader paradigm of ensuring access that must necessarily form the basis of future-focused acquisitions competencies. Such a complex technologically mediated and rapidly changing environment requires a collaborative and outcome-focused approach rather than one that is purely process based.

REFERENCES

ALCTS. 1994. "Statement on Principles and Standards of Acquisitions Practice." Acquisitions Section Ethics Task Force. Available: www.ala.org/advocacy/proethics/explanatory/acquisitions.

Alderson, Carolyn. 2014. "Evidence Provides More Options for E-Book Acquisition." *Research Information*. 7 April 2014. Available: www.researchinformation.info/news/news_story.php?news_id=1556.

Arch, Xan. 2009. "RSS for Acq." *Against the Grain* 21, no. 2: 59–60.

Chapman, Liz. 2004. *Managing Acquisitions in Library and Information Services*, rev. ed. London: Facet.

Doctorow, Cory. 2008. *Content: Selected Essays on Technology, Creativity, and the Future of the Future*. San Francisco: Tachyon.

Holden, Jesse. 2013. "Charting Discovery." *Against the Grain* 25, no. 4: [1], 14.

Howard, David and Constance Wiebrands. 2011. "Culture Shock: Librarians' Response to Web Scale Search." *ECU Publications Pre*. Edith Cowan University Research Online. http://ro.ecu.edu.au/cgi/viewcontent.cgi?article=7208&context=ecuworks.

Manhoff, Marlene. 2006. "The Materiality of Digital Collections: Theoretical and Historical Perspectives." *portal: Libraries and the Academy* 6, no. 3: 311–325.

Pickett, Carmelita, Simona Tabacaru, and Jeanne Harrell. 2014. "E-Approval Plans in Research Libraries." *College & Research Libraries* 75, no. 2, March 2014: 218–231.

Pyle, Encarnacion. 2009. "OSU Book Winnowing Opposed." *Columbus Dispatch*, May 13, 2009. Available: www.dispatch.com/content/stories/local/2009/05/13/OSU_library.ART_ART_05-13-09_B1_ITDRI8J.html.

Smiraglia, Richard P. 2003. "The History of 'The Work' in the Modern Catalog." *Historical Aspects of Cataloging and Classification* 35, no. 3/4: 553–567.

Thatcher, Sanford G. 2009. "The Hidden Digital Revolution in Scholarly Publishing: POD, SRDP, the 'Long Tail,' and Open Access." *Against the Grain* 21, no. 2: 60–63.

Zhang, Ying. 2014. "Evidence-Based Acquisitions: A Win-Win?" *Information Today Europe*. April 6, 2014. Available: www.infotoday.eu/Articles/Editorial/Featured-Articles/Evidence-based-acquisitions-a-win-win-98610.aspx.

CHAPTER **FOUR**

Assemblages of Feedback and Service

eedback serves to reinforce or modify (and, hopefully, improve) habits, practices, and, ultimately, service. In other words, feedback tells whether a process or service is functioning as expected. Service, in turn, supports the user community and library mission, and should provide a mechanism for providing feedback for continual adaptation to the information ecosystem. A countless number of feedback mechanisms help us through our daily lives, and such mechanisms can be quite simple. These include biological ones, such as our senses. Feedback mechanisms can be mechanical, such as a thermometer to confirm the exact temperature; feedback mechanisms can also be personal, such as when someone complains about a service. Service, in turn, benefits from deliberate practice and constant attention. Service should be driven and enhanced by feedback, helping anticipate (as well as respond to) library needs and expectations. Together, a feedback-service dyad forms an assemblage, which in turn is an essential component of the larger acquisitions assemblage.

Service Role of Acquisitions

When one thinks of acquisitions, the content aspect is likely the most obvious one. While it may be true that acquisitions does, in fact, acquire content as part of the library's larger collection assemblage, the actual function of acquisitions goes well beyond the purchase of content. Acquisitions is a service-oriented unit of the library and serves the community of library users to the same degree that other areas of the library do. However, acquisitions has a kind of invisible aspect to it. While the idea of the physical collection remains the most tangible and likely the most pervasive symbol of the library, the service value added by acquisitions may not be as immediately apparent as the value added by other service areas of library such as reference, circulation, or even cataloging. Yet, bringing content into a library's assemblage of access (see chapters 2 and 3) adds a tremendous amount of value since sought-after content is otherwise unavailable and perhaps even unknown. While traditional elements of acquisitions were not as straightforward as simply "buying books," its transformation within the contemporary information environment is, likewise, not as simple as establishing access. Acquisitions, like all other parts of the library, is a service sector that adds value by acting on content and interacting with other parts of the library and the user community of which it is a part (and which it supports).

Libraries through the ages became very efficient at building and organizing physical collections of items. This ensured a certain availability of what was, hopefully, a critical mass of content that could be physically accessed when needed. When libraries consisted of physical items, collection-building was largely anticipatory. Physical items necessarily had to be identified, then moved in some kind of physical form to a physical location where a patron could, quite literally, pick an item up. Libraries functioned as some of the most efficient information-gathering machines of the previous, mechanical age. The collecting of books and journals, especially, as well as newspapers, microforms, and the indexes and abstracts that were required to locate specific pieces of information buried within these physical formats are ingenious methods of searching print-bound information. The nature of the content's physical container impacted all library services, certainly, and had significant implications for acquisitions—the personnel who dealt almost entirely with the container. Those tasked with locating content did not necessarily have to identify where information was printed, but had to discover where the objects were located. Looking at the library in terms of its physicality, some structural categories can be readily identified and used to help illustrate the various service areas:

1. *Highly subjective.* These assemblages focus primarily on content. While the container has access implications, the goal is to connect users to specific content. One example is collection development, where content is selected for the collection. When developing the collection, the first priority is to identify the content—the specific, organized information—that is needed. Content might include the text of a novel or the music from a particular composer. Typically, this identification of content has occurred simultaneously with the identification of an item (e.g., book or CD). The second part of the collection development function is selection of the content for the collection. Such a selection will be based on a number of factors (e.g., curricular need, user request, collection focus), but the selector ultimately will have a hypothetical end use in mind. This selection of content will likely continue to be tied to format (e.g., eBook or standard CD), but developing a collection—physical, virtual, or just-in-time—will foremost be concerned with content. Another example of a content-based function within the library is the provision of reference service. The goal of reference service is to first facilitate discovery of content and then help determine how to establish access. This is typically in response to an acute information need, where learning the information is of primary importance. The format, the vehicle to discovery, will be an essential consideration in terms of timely access, but is ultimately ancillary to the user's information needs.

2. *Highly structured.* These are assemblages within the library that rely on process and procedure. One example of a highly structured assemblage is circulation. The circulation process may first be defined in terms of policy, which defines what items circulate, for how long, and to whom. For example, a policy might indicate that all materials in a collection circulate except those designated as being part of reference or special collections. From the regime of general policies establishing the use of materials, specific procedures are established. Procedures may detail how a book is checked out, how the borrowing period is determined, and what penalties are invoked when a borrowing period is exceeded. A procedure

might specify that students may check out circulating books for 28 days or that faculty members may check out reference items for two days. The circulating of physical items is largely indifferent to the content; it is, rather, organized around the process of moving and tracking items through the library and user community.

A second process-based library assemblage is cataloging. Though catalogers interact with content on a general level, the procedure for cataloging library content into MARC format—and creating other kinds of metadata—is well established with national standards (e.g., Anglo-American Cataloguing Rules, Second Edition [AACR2] and Resource Description and Access [RDA]) that dictate how content objects should be treated generally. It is prescribed, for example, that the title is transcribed from the title page into the 245 field of the MARC record; transcription includes specific instructions for setting indicators, creating subfields, and even the use of capitalization and punctuation. Because the procedure is set for all catalogers, the local policies are derived from the universal procedure. Examples of local cataloging policy include identifying those situations when local notes are added to the record to enrich description or when additional custom fields of description are used to meet user needs. While intellectual reconfigurations of cataloging (e.g., Functional Requirements for Bibliographic Records [FRBR], linked data, etc.) confirm a shifting priority approach to cataloging within the broader information ecosystem, an approach that allows for a more nuanced and dynamic use of metadata, the function of cataloging itself has hitherto centered on structuring a process for description of content objects as an organizing principle. While subject heading assignment and classification are inextricably bound to the content, these practices are done within a framework focused on describing an object. The acquisition assemblage is especially constructed according to local processes, but it is not as rigidly tied to fixed process in the same way as access services or cataloging.

3. *Highly contingent.* This third category includes the acquisitions assemblage, as well as some others (e.g., archives, preservation, etc.). Acquisitions is semi-structured, working across diverse frameworks such as order records in the ILS, state and local tax codes, and collection development policies. At the same time, acquisitions work is relatively fluid: sourcing content, working with a variety of third-party entities, and responding to acute access needs (in all formats). While all aspects of

service within the contemporary library have been influenced by the item, the acquisitions function is uniquely centered on the item as a basic essence of its being—the item is, therefore, an ontological entity. What emerges in item-based acquisitions functions is a routine that starts with an item—assumed to be a physical entity—with all subsequent functions premised on that fact. Acquisitions has had to act on items in a unique way, where they were not primarily the manifestation of a procedure (generally) nor the embodiment of content (specifically). While the acquisition of content (in the form of content objects) is definitely part of acquisitions, interaction directly with content is not the organizing principle of the acquisitions assemblage.

Aspects of Service

As new formats continue to proliferate in the new information universe, adding objects even while neutralizing items, acquisitions needs to reposition itself conceptually within the information universe and func- tionally in the library. Part of the complexity is that physical items continue to exist within the collection, and as potential objects to be acquired. In specific cases, such as rare book collections, physical items even maintain their primacy. It may be, and likely should be, impossible to concentrate on physicality or format as a starting point for rethinking acquisitions. Rather, conceptions of service should be framed in acquisitions according to new demands by patrons and the supply of content. Rick Anderson, for example, has made the case for developing patron-centered practices that become possible in acquisitions with the erosion between technical and public services. He argues that any approach to acquisitions must be thought of in terms of serving library users "*directly* by being flexible and responding to their changing needs" (Anderson, 2007: 190; emphasis original). Such changes in content production consumption are driving changes in the organization of acquisitions, too, leading to a range of responses when reorganizing technical services. Adaptation might involve any number of changes. One such change might result in reimagining the acquisitions librarian as the e-resources librarian, if appropriate to the mission of the library, the content being acquired, and the time needed to manage various resources. Other, more drastic responses might result in merging acquisitions with other library units or disbanding the formal acquisitions unit altogether in favor of a more streamlined or integrated technical services organization (Lopatin, 2004). Unless the library is foregoing all continuing and new acquisitions, however, the professional competency of acquisitions must reside somewhere in the organization and be readily identifiable. No matter the response to the growing instability within the new information universe, acquisitions work is only getting more complicated. Acquisitions functions must be reevaluated as its own discrete element of overall library services no matter how the functions of acquiring content are ultimately manifested organizationally.

The most important aspect of reconsidering acquisitions as a function (as opposed to acquisitions as an organizational unit) is to ensure that the function is defined in terms of service rather than process. In fact, no matter how the tasks are divided, it is important to define what exactly is being designated as acquisitions work. A key in this approach is to note that due to the organizational contingencies mentioned above, it may be impossible to define things that acquisitions does that no other service or administrative unit in the library or the university might do; indeed, acquisitions may do all of these or none (in the cases where there is no separate acquisitions unit).

POTENTIAL ACCESS

Acquisitions foremost provides the potential for access, and may achieve this in many ways. It is important to note that collection development defines access needs, cataloging creates the pathway for access, reference creates the interface for access, and access services brokers or mediates the access. This potential for access is generated in a number of functions, such as the following:

- Managing vendor relationships
- Placing, tracking, and following up on orders
- Reviewing, transmitting, and filing licenses
- Receiving orders and establishing access to e-resources
- Monitoring the budget and reporting balances
- Paying invoices, balancing credit card statements, and
- Processing seller-issued credits

As described in chapter 3, acquisitions actively creates an assemblage of access that has traditionally been considered to be the collection—those items that are owned by the institution. However, the sphere of access might include virtual electronic resources to which the library has access or other content that is mediated by the library but not added to a permanent collection.

With access to content as a central goal, service from the library can be modeled in terms of access. When such an assemblage is created, the traditional notion of the supply chain or static channel of information dissemination breaks down. While the model of the supply chain still retains some use in particular cases, content that is object rather than item driven is not as fixed and can be acted on in different ways. In most circumstances, it can be useful to conceptualize the contemporary access assemblage as being like a network rather than fixed and distinct, with predetermined paths to follow in connecting with content. An approach embedding acquisitions within the library's larger service assemblage along with other units of the library emphasizes a shared approach to providing access, while leveraging the distinct skills and unique perspectives of each. Such a model underscores the breakdown of fixed boundaries between traditional library units already well underway (Bosch, Promis, and Sugnet, 2005). Such a service imperative drives a collaborative approach to acquisitions whether it is the immediate curricular needs of the liberal arts environment or the long-term, subject-intensive needs of the research environment.

More than ever, the conception of service as part of the acquisitions function should be framed foremost according to new demands created by the diversity of student, faculty, and researcher needs and expectations. This suggests a fluid notion of content that meets these new demands with a nuanced supply of information available from a field potential of formats. While acquisitions professionals still must hold to the standard that they strive "consistently for knowledge of the publishing and bookselling industry" (ALCTS, 1994, Statement 10), complete knowledge of publishing output is not possible. Instead, acquisitions practitioners must be ready to locate content through the tools at hand such as vendors (including approval plans), sophisticated use of the Web, and the assistance of innovative colleagues. Acquisitions must be able to meet access needs of information age library users by bringing necessary information objects into the library's access assemblage.

Integrating Assemblages

The current state of publishing has created a paradox. On the one hand, mainstream search technologies such as those provided by, Amazon, Apple, Google, and Microsoft, as well as other full-text search products seem to be rapidly disintermediating information seeking at all levels. Almost anyone can enter some keywords and generate a somewhat usable list of results, whether using a free online search engine or an expensive, library-supported discovery service. At the same time, the vastly complex information ecosystem is so content-dense and, at times, chaotic that even experienced information seekers find themselves quickly overwhelmed. At once there is both a plethora of information that can be found almost immediately and, simultaneously, a huge amount of information that may remain elusive even after several refined searches (whether because it is not indexed by a search engine, locked behind a **pay wall**, buried in a results list, or any number of possible reasons).

The role of the acquisition professional has been reasserted within this new landscape where information "noise" may seem everywhere while sought-after content proves elusive. This postmodern information ecology has posed challenges across the entire library. Acquisitions is actually called to mediate in two distinct parts of the access process. In the first instance, acquisitions practitioners increasingly must be able to identify the location—real or virtual—of more content, from more sources, and in a variety of formats. In the second instance, acquisitions practitioners increasingly may need to maintain the access after it has been successfully established. The latter situation was represented to a degree when all content was in a physical format: acquisitions practitioners would often have to replace lost materials or add additional copies of extremely popular material. However, this was a relatively rare occurrence and, being merely an extension of a general acquisition program, was easily incorporated into existing workflows. But now in addition to physical items, electronic resources create an added layer of technology in the form of resource management software (possibly including an ERM, link resolver, or discovery service) as well as networked access that likely require active upkeep and troubleshooting.

To provide an excellent end-user experience, successful disinter-mediated access actually requires a high degree of mediation behind the scenes. The function of acquisitions within the library has expanded and is now a technology-driven, multivalent task. Where access within the acquisitions unit was previously generated through a number of essentially clerical functions—phone calls, mail order, faxes, and filing—the role of acquisitions is now complicated by expectations of around-the-clock, real-time access to an information base many times larger than anything that could be imagined before the dawning of the Information Age. It is impossible now to remove the practice of acquiring content from the practice of providing information service to library users. These aspects of service create the first half of a two-part cycle, where service is directly tied to library user needs in real time, and user needs in real time reinforce aspects of service.

The multiple routes available to content require heavily mediated access controls. A suite of software tools may be used by acquisitions to maintain access, including the following:

- Integrated library system (ILS)
- Electronic resource management system (ERMS)
- A-to-Z list or other publication indexing tool
- Link resolver
- Vendor or publisher content management platform
- Discovery service
- Statistical analysis
- Local institutional repository (IR)
- Digital archive, such as LOCKSS (Lots of Copies Keep Stuff Safe) or Portico

These electronic tools have many forms and often require complex, technical, and even proprietary specifications to run. It may be that acquisitions administers all, some, none, or just parts of these systems. Most of these systems will be implemented and run in close collaboration with the library systems unit or the organization's information technology department. However, the information that goes into and comes out of these systems will inevitably involve acquisitions once they are in place. Because these information systems are implemented to manage the content that the library has access to, data concerning acquisitions details—such as payment amount, license terms, package content, and consortial agreements—will inevitably be needed for system enrichment or reporting. A critical consideration when developing, evaluating, streamlining, or updating an acquisitions unit or its workflow is knowing how these tools can be used, if at all, in improving service to library users as provided by acquisitions. Such an evaluation will be site specific, determined in part by local needs and availability of resources.

Staffing

Acquisitions is an assemblage not only of workflows and technology, but of people as well. Acquisitions staff constitute part of the larger service assemblage of the library and are therefore a critical piece of the feedback loop. The acquisitions assemblage can be organized and scaled many ways. In smaller libraries, acquisitions responsibilities may be handled by only a single person. In larger organizations, responsibilities may be divided by format (print and electronic), order type (firm order or continuation), or function (order, receive, and pay). Construction of the acquisitions assemblage may depend on many factors, such as personal knowledge and skills, the kinds of content a library acquires, or even the physical location and layout of the library.

Despite the relatively simple schemas that may represent acquisitions on an organizational chart, assemblages are often more nuanced than they seem. While organization is important for managing people and workflows, individual competencies and skills will vary from library to library and person to person. It is important that organizational charts are truly representative, mapping competencies and information. Boxes on a page should not completely define (and therefore restrict) people's contribution; rather, the boxes on the page should map the nodes of expertise and knowledge present within the library.

As the nature of acquisitions changes, so too do staffing needs. The state of constant change now inherent within the information ecosystem must become a part of a library's organizational assemblage. "Organizations are in a constant state of change and rate of change will vary from organization to organization," says Goodman and Loh (2011: 242). "It is important to recognize that all change involves people: what they do and/ or how they do it" (Ibid.). Acquisitions staff routinely navigate not only changes in library organization and technology, but changes external to the library and its immediate community of users, such as those in publishing and even the global economy. This flux impacts not only numbers of staff but what staff does, and the impact is felt in both monograph and serials acquisitions. Glasser, for instance, observes regarding the "complex, non-linear world of e-serials": "As electronic serials continue to rapidly replace their print counterpart, the traditional print management activities such as check-in, claiming, open stacks maintenance, and binding have come into question or have naturally diminished" (2010: 143). These changes in content focus, workflows, and technical competencies may result in either the reduction of staff or the need for current staff members to develop new skills to keep an acquisitions unit moving forward.

Technology

Technology-driven tools contribute just as much to the changing nature of acquisitions work as does the changing nature of information itself. And just as a nuanced understanding of formats is required to adequately respond to library user needs, technical expertise is required to successfully manage an acquisitions program. The biggest impact, perhaps, is the concentration of work in higher-level positions. Tasks that once could be delegated to entry-level paraprofessionals or detail-oriented students, including transmission of orders, processing claims, or entering payment information, are increasingly automated by way of complex software. This is true not only for the ILS but for some of the other systems that may fall to acquisitions, such as a link resolver or discovery service. Various resource management systems, from the vendor's online ordering system to an electronic resource management system (ERMS) to the ILS and discovery service, may be hosted in the cloud but assigned a local administrator in the library. These systems may in turn interface with other local and cloud-based library systems to deliver MARC records, receive orders, or transmit invoice and payment data. In some cases, the acquisitions professional will need to partner closely with the systems librarian or even the organization's information technology (IT) office. Of course, the technological knowledge may reside in acquisitions, streamlining part of the process.

Any system that acquisitions uses to manage content objects, orders, or invoices will require some kind of trade-off. Sometimes this can be as simple as getting detailed training to maximize the use of the system. Other times, it can require establishing relationships both within and outside of the library to ensure an appropriate level of technical support.

In all cases, the impact of implementation or migration of any management system will likely have to be presented to colleagues and administrators in ways that demonstrate added value. Value can be determined many ways, but savings (e.g., time or money) or enhanced service (e.g., reduced time between ordering and access) are two ways to measure the value of a technology tool. (See sidebar, "Measuring Value.")

MEASURING VALUE

Moving to a new technology—whether implementing something completely new or migrating to something newer—is a process that is likely to draw on a library's financial and personnel resources. Though often new systems or upgraded versions are taken for granted as part of working within a technology-driven environment, decisions to move from one technology to another should be part of a strategy to enhance value of library services to the user community. Some aspects to consider in acquisitions:

- Can the new technology save time?
- Will the new technology provide an adequate **audit trail** for expenditures?
- Is the new interface easier to use?

Because of its ubiquity, the ILS is likely to be familiar to most library personnel no matter where in the organization they work. Still occasionally referred to erroneously as the online catalog (which actually forms just one part of the ILS), these systems continue to be the primary system of record for acquisitions work in those libraries where they have been set up. Though not all libraries use an ILS to manage the acquisitions process, such a system can leverage technology to organize, integrate, and streamline essential acquisitions functions. The ILS facilitates four critical acquisitions functions: placing and maintaining orders, recording receipt and access information, tracking payments and funds, and storing vendor information. In cases where acquisitions adds and maintains bibliographic records, interaction with and input into the ILS will be even more extensive. Since it is the system from which the user-facing online catalog is generated, it is the logical place to track the ordering and receipt of orders for content purchased or leased by the library.

Along with metadata for content and the associated orders that acquisitions is working with, vendor and fund information is usually maintained in the ILS as well. At its most basic, the ILS improves upon a file-based strategy for managing orders, a Rolodex-based system for tracking vendor contact information, and a calculator-based technology for tracking fund information. But strategically, the ILS needs to be conceived of, and subsequently utilized, beyond basic information storage. The contemporary ILS, whether commercial or open source, is a dynamic database that provides powerful tracking and reporting capabilities that frequently can be automated, at least to a degree. Automating the ILS where possible can absorb redundant tasks, such as creating online orders or entering invoice data, and free up time to address more difficult problems.

With the vast amount of data entered into the ILS, reporting can provide valuable feedback as the annual budget cycle progresses. Reports showing open orders (those orders not yet received) or fund balances can be a key point of collaboration with personnel in collection development to manage the budget. Information about open orders can be used by acquisitions to provide critical feedback to vendors about the latter's service to the library. Other reports may be possible, such as those showing the average time it takes an order to be fulfilled after being transmitted to the vendor. The ILS provides great value not only by storing acquisitions data but by supplying critical feedback in real time.

The ERMS was developed to fill a resource management need not met by the traditional ILS—even in those systems with a robust acquisitions module. The reason is that the management of electronic resource acquisition processes is often more complicated than can be effectively handled by the traditional ILS. The ERMS evolved out of the spreadsheets and paper files that librarians started in order to track those things that could not be added and tracked systematically in the ILS: license terms, service inquiries, access requirements, use restrictions, and renewal dates. ERMS have been developed by major commercial ILS vendors, content vendors, and open source initiatives. Most are intended to be used as separate modules, though increasingly "ERMS" functionality is integrated either in "next-gen" ILS technology or cloud-based vendor-supplied content management systems (see below). Of course, an ERMS that "matches" a library's ILS may more fully integrate the two databases of information. In particular, the ability to have the financial information shared by both systems is what makes the addition of an ERMS particularly useful. Frequently, however, integrating financial and subscription data from the two systems presents a large challenge and can severely limit the utility of a stand-alone ERMS. Another consideration in starting up an ERMS alongside the ILS is the sheer amount of time it takes to get electronic resource data—especially license terms—entered into the ERMS. The ERMS will, in the final analysis, only be as good as the data that have been put into it. This alone restricts the number of libraries that can afford to get an ERMS fully functional.

A promising solution for managing electronic resources is agent-supplied online systems. Basically extensions of current online agent databases (e.g., EBSCONET, OttoSerials, etc.), such systems offer similar advantages to those online systems developed by large monographic vendors (e.g., Coutts' OASIS and YBP's GOBI). Like monographic acquisitions (including firm, standing, and approval orders) which can be effectively and efficiently managed through a given vendor's online system, subscription agents' online systems may prove to be the best way to keep on top of electronic resource orders of all kinds, including e-journals, packages, and consortial purchases. While the role of the serial agents was seriously in doubt when publisher-direct packages and publisher-bundled "Big Deals" seemed to be the direction of journal publishing, the importance of agent-mediated subscription is becoming clear (see sidebar, "Big Deals"). Subscription agents already possess a large amount of pertinent subscription information within their own data-bases, such as pricing, subscription periods, up-to-date publisher contact information, and claiming history, all of which makes subsequent tracking of this information redundant if the library is merely reentering the data. Though not as robust as a stand-alone ERMS module, such agent-based subscription management systems can provide a convenient and economical means of tracking e-resources along with print subscriptions.

Such a system is not a panacea. For one, by relying on such a vendor system, the library must essentially depend on the vendor to maintain the system and provide continuous, reliable access. This may not matter, as much of the same monograph data has been similarly outsourced (perhaps to an even greater extent) through vendor online databases. Information does get back to the library in terms of renewal lists and invoices. However, if the subscription and consortial management data were to be tracked

BIG DEALS

According to Frazier (2001): "Simply put, the Big Deal is an online aggregation of journals that publishers offer as a one-price, one-size-fits-all package." Initially, the Big Deal provided a means for libraries to acquire a large bundle of titles from a given publisher at a relatively low per-title cost when compared to subscribing to individual (or "a la carte") titles. In aggregate, "Big Deals offered, at slightly greater costs, much more access to journal literature. But the prices for those deals provided a new base for escalation in the cost of journals that is higher than inflation in the rest of the economy and greater than increases in library acquisitions budgets" (Blecic, et al., 2013: 191). In other words, the Big Deal seemed to provide one strategy for getting around the rising cost of journal subscriptions, but ultimately did not offer the sustainable solution that libraries were looking for.

Part of the affirmation of the agent's role is due to pushback on some of the limitations embedded in the publisher-direct Big Deal model. While acknowledging that "libraries gain access to many journals with Big Deal agreements," Pickett (2011) concludes that "some drawbacks include the time required to complete title reconciliation, restrictive title-level cancellations, and additional fees to subscribe to new and acquired journals that become available during the multi-year agreement" (260). A few Big Deals (or in some cases, even just a single one) can tie up a large percentage of a library's acquisition budget and limit the ability to acquire content beyond the licensed bundle—or even limit the flexibility to change a given mix of titles. Subscribing directly or through an agent, though often increasing cost per journal subscription, may provide some flexibility—but likely will reduce the amount of content overall that a library can subscribe to. In the face of tightening budgets and rising journal costs, libraries are faced with a difficult decision.

---

through a given vendor, the library would be tied to that vendor. While not requiring a business relationship that goes on ad infinitum, the implications for changing vendors in this circumstance would be significant. Though it may be possible to use emerging standards for electronic management systems standards to walk data from a vendor's database to the library's ERMS, an agreement should be worked out ahead of time with the vendor to ensure the portability of the library's data. Also, some organizations may not allow their data to be hosted by a third party. In that case, the library might be required to purchase an ERMS that can be maintained on site if such functionality is important to managing access to e-resources. An open source system may be an option that provides initial cost savings and local control, but also places the burden of implementation, maintenance, and support within the library.

DO YOU NEED AN ERMS?

It may seem that an electronic resource management system (ERMS) will solve much of the work and streamline much of the processing that goes into acquiring and managing electronic resources. Especially in acquisitions, where securing access has become quite complicated for many resources, a technological tool that promises the possibility of organization and streamlining may be quite tempting.

As with many technologies, an ERMS will not automatically simplify the e-resource management complications that seem to appear at every stage of the process.

Some goals to identify at the start of the evaluation process include the following:

- What functions will the ERMS need to have to save time in acquisitions?
- What are the technical limitations of any ERMS under consideration?
- What technical expertise is available within your organization? How will individuals contribute to overall implementation and maintenance? If the ERMS under consideration is open source, is there time and expertise available within the organization to support the system?
- To what extent will the ERMS need to interact with your ILS?
- How exactly how will the ERMS support the acquisitions workflow? Additionally, how could an ERMS potentially support other areas of the library (e.g., collection development, access services, etc.)?
- What people or units outside acquisitions will need access to the ERMS? How will the system be administered?
- What are the experiences of other libraries with the systems being considered?

■ What level of customer support is available from the ERMS
provider? If the ERMS under consideration is open source,
is a process in place to communicate problems and develop
solutions both before and after implementation?

Keep in mind that the ERMS is likely to be just one system supporting just
one part of the library's acquisitions functions. The trade-offs must be carefully
considered and the decision to invest an organization's time and money in the
implementation and maintenance of such a system must be made only when an
ERMS will result in a net savings.

Some questions to have in mind before going ahead with buying and
implementing an ERMS are these:

■ Will the cost of purchase and ongoing maintenance take away
from other products or services that could simplify or improve
the work being done in acquisitions?

■ Does the added value from working with an ERMS justify the
cost of the product and its upkeep?

■ Is there a critical mass of e-resources that justifies the need
for a specialized management system?

Like any tool, the ERMS will be helpful to a widely varying degree. Determining
organizational need, available resources for implementation and support, and
the long-term plan for integrating the ERMS into the acquisitions function will
ensure that use of the system is appropriate and productive.

Given the large number of databases and inevitable overlap of
holdings a library is likely to have, other systems have emerged to help
manage access. While not necessarily designed specifically for management of acquisitions processes or for use exclusively by an acquisitions
unit, these systems are an almost ubiquitous part of the access regime and
acquisitions professionals will need to have some familiarity with them.
The **A-to-Z list** provides a relatively simple approach to accessing journals
and/or databases via an online listing of and linking to current titles.
These assemblages of titles can usually be generated automatically from
the library's holdings (usually via the *knowledgebase*; see below). Recently,
other holdings management tools (such as EBSCO's *Full Text Finder*)
have emerged that provide a more dynamic management approach to
the library's collection of content objects and index data that is available

electronically. A **link resolver** allows the library user to collocate and access all instances of specific content available from one or more online sources on the fly. Since identical content may be available from multiple sources, a link resolver creates a shortcut to identifying and accessing overlapping content; the library is even able to link directly to full text contained in a preferred source, saving the user the additional step of identifying a particular source from a list of many.

In order to identify accessible titles, the library activates (manually and/or automatically) their own holdings via a **knowledgebase** (KB). The KB is essentially a vast index of possible available titles, from which the library selects their acquired content as "targets" for potential linking. Frequently, maintenance of the holdings in a library's KB is performed by the acquisitions staff, who take a more direct role in managing access than in a print-centric environment. The KB is typically provided by a third-party entity, and may be either a commercial or open-source product. Many library users rely on the link resolver and knowledgebase without even being aware of their existence, and acquisitions staff actively works to keep access functioning seamlessly.

This linking technology—an assemblage all on its own—uses the **OpenURL** format in conjunction with a knowledgebase to mediate between a user search and the relevant content available through the library. The standard for the OpenURL Framework is set out by the National Information Standards Organization (NISO, 2010), which defines the structure for "obtaining context-sensitive services pertaining the referenced resource" (1). In other words, the relevant sources of the desired content-object available to the user is identified through the OpenURL itself via the link resolver. The library therefore need not maintain myriad direct links to authorized content from authorized users, but can generate a list of services from the OpenURL (Apps and MacIntyre, 2006). The services provided through the resolver include not only full text, but also library catalog records and even links to ILL.

Finally, the discovery service, as discussed in chapter 3, is a technology that enables a library user to run a given search simultaneously across many information resources (e.g., the library catalog, databases, journal platforms, eBooks, etc.) to decrease search time, collocate results, and link to full text where available. As described by Breeding (2014):

Discovery service providers must create a technical infrastructure capable of supporting these massive indexes and develop interfaces that patrons use to search and gain access to the content items. These large-scale platforms require significant investments in technology infrastructure, software development, and human and automated processes for populating and maintaining the indexes. The cost and resource allocation needed to create one of these web-scale discovery services exceed what would be feasible for a single library or most library consortia (14).

Discovery services incorporate many different, integral technological components, and the link resolver and KB both are critical parts of this complex assemblage. However, due to the intricacy of the discovery assemblage, a well-developed discovery service can potentially improve on OpenURL-linking alone (Brooks, 2013). By using sophisticated indexing, customizable interfaces, and dynamic link resolving, discovery services have also superseded federated searching. In a federated search, terms entered into a single interface are mapped into two or more native interfaces to run, ostensibly, the same search across multiple platforms at once, often with less than ideal results. Because discovery services, by contrast, utilize centralized indexing and a KB of known content rather than parallel searches running simultaneously, they return results faster, more accurately, and more consistently. It is likely that the acquisitions unit will play a key role in ensuring that the library's holdings reflected in the KB are up to date and accurate, especially as new orders are placed and annual renewals are processed.

While none of these technologies may be directly part of an acquisitions function, access considerations permeate all aspects of the overarching library service mission. It is possible that any number of the acquisitions functions will incorporate, or at least intersect, with one or more of these technologies. For libraries that offer access to large amounts of online content, these management tools are a critical part of service. As the service imperative increases for acquisitions, knowing how content can be managed to best provide routes to access for end users is a critical aspect of the function.

Content Acquisition Plans

The process of selecting and acquiring content is fairly systematic in most libraries: content decisions are based on local requirements for subject coverage, content level, format, and language. To support access to this selected content, acquisitions designs workflows for making content accessible and develops relationships with content providers (like publishers and vendors) to facilitate acquisition of the prescribed content. One way to expedite the selection-to-acquisition process and free up staff time is by establishing various kinds of plans to automate this process.

One of the most recognized and institutionalized "plan assemblages" is the approval plan, where books are identified and provided to the library according to a detailed profile (see chapter 3). Though subject to the vicissitudes of the publishing market from year to year, approval plans comprise a relatively predictable model for budgeting and acquisitions. The feedback mechanisms here are fairly predictable, as well: the parameters are well defined and granular. The feedback, though, mostly comes through subject selectors and circulation statistics. This feedback may therefore be general and even inaccurate.

Emerging out of a combination of a profile modeled on the traditional approval plan profile coupled with the technological possibilities of eBooks is the "patron-" or "**demand-driven acquisitions**" (DDA) model. In this model, a pool of available titles made available for discovery—either through the catalog, discovery service, or both—are purchased based on use. DDA plans have become widely adopted in recent years (see Arch, 2011; Morris & Siebert, 2011: 105–106).

Like an approval plan, DDA relies on a collaboration between librarians and vendors to determine a list of accessible titles available for usage-based purchase (the title "pool"). Creation and updating of the pool is based around a profile, similar to an instrument that would be used to create an approval plan. Titles are made available be adding records with hyperlinks to the catalog, activating titles through the discovery service, or both. The eBooks in the DDA discovery pool are accessible just like any other eBook resource that the library makes available, and the user does not know if their access triggers an expense for the library. Use of an eBook title in the DDA pool may trigger an immediate purchase of the book or may result in a **short-term loan** (STL). An STL allows temporary access to a title for a percentage of the book's purchase cost; however, these STL charges do not generally count towards the purchase price. In a model that incorporates STLs, a purchase is automatically triggered after a certain number of loans. This results in a higher cost per book permanently acquired, but reduces the overall number of purchases.

DDA plans are especially popular as a tool for saving libraries money without sacrificing access. Because both DDA and approval plans are profile-based collaborations with a vendor, it is even possible to merge the two types of plan into one hybrid model: the DDA-preferred approval plan (Roll, 2016). In her case study of this model, Roll concludes that "[a] lthough some libraries have taken an either/or approach to approval plans and DDA, a harmony of the two methods can ensure access to needed monographs despite the limitations of cost and format" (10). Such a model capitalizes on the inherent efficiency and flexibility of profiles, coupled with technical possibilities offered by integrated online systems and e-formats. The expanded profile assemblage makes it possible to bring the more traditional mechanisms of a just-in-case print approval plan with the much wider, user-centric net cast by a dynamic DDA plan.

But several ethical components come into play with the assemblage that constitutes the DDA model. Leveraging technology to provide anytime discovery, real-time access, and user-driven purchasing has been disruptive to both libraries and publishers. On the library side, the question of increasingly providing access to content without the security of permanent access is an important one. Libraries—along with other cultural institutions such as museums—are important repositories of information, and just-in-time access assemblages like DDA can undercut a library's mission to preserve content. On the publisher side, the economic model that supports publishing can be undercut by uncertain or even shrinking revenues from book sales. Seger and Allen (2011), writing from a publisher's perspective, are ambivalent about the impact of DDA on the information marketplace. While acknowledging that "the notion of paying only for books that get real, demonstrated use makes sense in today's climate" (32), they point out that:

> [f]rom the publisher's perspective, to survive in a patron-driven world, we have to excel in driving users to our content, and there is ample opportunity to do that. But there remain a host of questions. Challenges to the finances of monograph publishers

> as they adapt to a post-approval plan world will shape the future
> publishing programs as more and more scholarly programs ac-
> cept e[lectronic] as their primary format for monographs (34).

While presenting users with the most access in the most economical fashion, DDA poses challenges to the information ecosystem: it has the potential to undermine a traditional library function (i.e., title-by-title selection), on the one hand, while undercutting publisher revenue on the other. In fact, publishers have already responded to the drastic market change by increasing prices of DDA titles and extending embargoes before they become available (Cramer, 2016) At the same time, DDA may provide an opportunity for publishers. Goedeken and Lawson (2015) affirm that direct involvement of the user via DDA is a really "disruptive innovation" (218). Libraries not only facilitate connecting users to content but also ensure that stable, quality publications are easily discoverable. The ethical and economic question of DDA in the information marketplace needs to be an ongoing conversation among all the stakeholders.

Mechanisms of Feedback

Along with the ever-increasing assemblages of access, ever-expanding assemblages of feedback have proliferated throughout both technological and cultural space. The mechanisms of feedback have become familiar through their ubiquity; such mechanisms now permeate daily life. Feedback is an essential component of social media; it is frequently integrated within retail and auction Web sites, solicited through online surveys, and even requested on fast food receipts. E-mail and social networking provide a constant flow of communication between peers and colleagues, and with it a barrage of feedback information. Libraries rely on feedback from informal Web forms and questionnaires to highly specialized survey instruments such as the Association of Research Libraries' LibQUAL+ (www.libqual.org). These mechanisms come together in a feedback assemblage, combining locally. This localized feedback assemblage serves a regulating function for *services* provided by and through the library, and the increasingly numerous and anonymized *relationships* moderated through the online environment via online searching, access, and communication. Like access to information generally speaking, the ability to procure services and establish relationships is now more diffuse than ever, and the need has arrived to manage due to abundance rather than stockpile due to scarcity.

In conjunction with assemblages of access, assemblages of feedback serve to more fully and intentionally integrate acquisitions into the broader service mission of the library. Increasingly automated mechanisms will loop feedback to or through acquisitions from a number of locations (real and virtual) within the information ecosystem. One critical aspect of converting mechanized feedback into a dynamic element of service from acquisitions is knowing what feedback is available, what it implies about service, and how such feedback can ultimately improve the role of acquisitions within the library information and service environment. Online forms for reporting service outages and usage statistics automatically gathered through e-resource usage represent just two possibilities of feedback mechanisms that can inform the acquisitions process. Additional to informing acquisitions, increasing amounts of feedback will connect acquisitions to other processes and functions throughout the library (such as cataloging, ILL, circulation, etc.).

The electronic systems used to manage acquisitions processes also provide an abundance of data about use. Of course, the very notion of "use" is problematic: the very definition of the term determines parameters for what constitutes a use, or many uses, and becomes a strategic decision. What is important to keep in mind is that what "use" is typically assumed to be indicative of is actually usefulness or, conversely, need. Therefore, care must be taken when reviewing any kind of use data to make sure that such data are meaningful within the context where they are gathered. One such initiative to improve this data is Project COUNTER:

Launched in March 2002, COUNTER (Counting Online Usage of Networked Electronic Resources) is an international initiative serving librarians, publishers and intermediaries by setting standards that facilitate the recording and reporting of online usage statistics in a consistent, credible, and compatible way. The first COUNTER Code of Practice, covering online journals and databases, was published in 2003. COUNTER's coverage was extended further with the launch of the Code of Practice for online books and reference works in 2006. The body of COUNTER compliant usage statistics has steadily grown as more and more vendors have adopted the COUNTER Codes of Practice. This has contributed to the new discipline of usage bibliometrics and a great deal of work is underway to try to establish "value metrics" associated with usage, in which the COUNTER compliant statistics play an increasingly important role (www.projectcounter.org/about.html).

While usage was formerly dependent on circulation and in-house browse statistics, the ability to track and report online usage significantly increases knowledge of how resources are being used. Pesch (2011) notes that:

> Usage statistics are playing an increasingly important role in helping librarians make collection management decisions. As acquisitions budgets for library collections become pre-dominately focused on electronic resources, librarians need a reliable means of analyzing the value of the various components of their collection. Project COUNTER (Counting Online Usage of Networked Electronic Resources) Code of Practice has become the standard for usage reporting and Standardized Usage Statistics Harvesting Initiative (SUSHI) is now being expected to remove much of the effort of retrieving these reports (353–354).

However, Pesch (2015) also notes that years after its introduction to the library community, confusion remains regarding how to implement SUSHI. While automating usage remains an important function often managed by acquisitions, technical hurdles still have yet to be overcome before the full potential of this automation is realized.

Automated feedback can provide a wealth of information to acquisitions. It is important that at every stage feedback informs acquisitions in such a way that decisions are made strategically and ethically. Feedback from the acquisitions and access processes must be incorporated in a contextual manner, and in a way that protects user anonymity. In their discussion of user privacy, vanDuinkerken, Kaspar, and Harrell note: As acquisitions work increasingly engages with electronic resources, a corresponding need for "policies and procedures surrounding proxy servers and individual authentication as well as the log files that record access" likewise arises (2014: 61). Data generated from content management systems, such as usage statistics or inventory updates, must inform decisions rather than dictate them, and must consolidate this information without comprising user privacy.

This detailed feedback is important not just for selecting content, but also for informing the acquisitions process—identifying what formats are available, where the content can be sourced from, and what access options (if any) to choose from. The fact that a title is out of print in paperback, for example, does not necessarily mean that the content is unavailable. Instead, it is imperative to engage feedback information in a critical way at the point where it reaches acquisitions.

Conclusion: Cycles of Feedback and Service

The cycle of feedback and service, which can be thought of as a continuous loop, is more intricate, granular, and pervasive than ever before. Forming an essential bridge between the publishing and library assemblages, acquisitions acts from within this continuous loop of feedback and service. Direct and active involvement with and within this cycle results in productive results and increased effectiveness, in terms of both more responsive service and more efficient workflows. Such engagement by the entire acquisitions unit—whether it is composed of one or several practitioners—is also in keeping with the standard of practice to "establish practical and efficient methods for the conduct of his/her office" (ALCTS, 1994, Statement 11). In particular, the enhanced role of acquisitions as a service unit within both the practice and mission of the library is an effect of information derived from this loop. A the same time, feedback through usage data, profile-driven purchasing, and even budgetary allocations (see chapter 5) makes it possible to constantly adjust and improve service.

Traditional notions of feedback and service were developed along the fixed channels that necessarily organized an analog information environment. Such channels make it difficult for acquisitions to act in a responsive way. A more useful model is one in which access and feedback are a continuous and ubiquitous loop comprising many sources within a larger assemblage. Like an expanded conception of formats, thinking about a granular, nuanced, and interactive way of providing access and gathering feedback allows for a more relevant, malleable approach to providing service while performing the familiar acquisitions function.

It is clear that work in acquisitions is always becoming more nuanced and complex. The work, once comprised chiefly of clerical tasks such as typing and filing, is "concentrating up," that is, requiring a well-developed *technical* and *technological* skill set by an experienced staff that is prepared to adapt to changes in the ecosystem. The capacity to automate processes—combined with the reality of working within a diverse environment of increasing complexity—results in an acquisitions assemblage that is more difficult to implement and harder to define than ever before. Library usage can be tracked and compiled in a number of contexts, automating some of the content analysis, and removing some of the supposition and guesswork that augmented previous collection development efforts. This new level and intensity of data gathering may allow acquisitions to respond more immediately and directly to information needs. Surveys, distributed through a number of paths, have the potential to deal with concerns or ideas that relate directly to contemporary acquisitions functions—especially service aspects, such as response time or effectiveness. With more tasks that involve connecting both librarians and library users with content, the loop of establishing access and receiving feedback is a critical piece of the emerging acquisitions environment in the information ecosystem,

In general, the point-and-click culture of the Information Age has shaped a community of library users that are more cognizant of the acquisitions process, if less understanding of it. Therefore, service exposure—direct contact between acquisitions practitioners and the library user community—has increased for acquisitions practitioners. This direct connection is now part of acquisitions' contemporary role in the library. E-access has put a burden of technological implementation, deployment, and ongoing maintenance on acquisitions. Technology has in some cases led to unreal expectations that parallel the new possibilities that same technology has created. The idea that everything is available on the Internet makes any delivery time more than instantaneous access seem like a delay. While a digital text might be delivered around the world in seconds, it might take days for a physical book to move across the state. The emerging publishing assemblage is increasing the number of potential formats, and allows for more routes to access while also embedding more mechanisms of feedback. This environment creates the possibility of closer collaboration with other assemblages within the library, such as collection development and access services, and allows for better responsiveness to user needs. Meeting these new expectations can be done through collaboration within the library, user community, and beyond. Reaching out to other acquisitions librarians with both counsel and assistance is an important principle of the profession (ALCTS, 1994, Statement 12), and takes on more importance as the information ecosystem becomes more expansive, service becomes increasingly complicated, and feedback becomes more ubiquitous.

REFERENCES

ALCTS. 1994. "Statement on Principles and Standards of Acquisitions Practice." Acquisitions Section Ethics Task Force. Available: www.ala.org/ala/mgrps/divs/alcts/resources/collect/acq/acqethics.

Anderson, Rick. 2007. "It's Not about the Workflow: Patron-Centered Practices for 21st-Century Serialists." *The Serials Librarian* 51, no. 3/4: 189–199.

Apps, Ann and Ross MacIntyre. 2006. "Why OpenURL?" *D-Lib Magazine* 12, no. 5. Available: www.dlib.org/dlib/may06/apps/05apps.html.

Arch, Xan. 2011. "Patron-Driven Acquisitions." *Against the Grain* 23, no. 3: [1].

Blecic, Deborah D., Stephen E. Wiberley Jr., Joan B. Fiscella, Sara Bahnmaier-Blaszczak, and Rebecca Lowery. 2013. "Deal or No Deal? Evaluating Big Deals and Their Journals." *College & Research Libraries* 74, no. 2: 178–194.

Bosch, Stephen, Patricia Promis, and Chris Sugnet. 2005. *Guide to Licensing and Acquiring Electronic Information.* Lanham, MD: Scarecrow Press.

Breeding, Marshall. 2014. "Discovery Product Functionality." *Library Technology Reports* 50, no. 1: 5–32.

Brooks, Sam. 2013. "Discovery: It's About the End User." *Against the Grain* 25, no. 2: 18.

COUNTER. n.d. "About COUNTER." Available: www.projectcounter.org/about.

Cramer, Carol Joyce. 2016. "Alternatives to Demand-Driven Acquisition: An Exploration of Opportunity Costs." *Against the Grain* 28, no. 2: 20–23.

Frazier, Kenneth. 2001."The Librarians' Dilemma: Contemplating the Cost of the 'Big Deal'." *D-Lib Magazine* 7, no. 3. Available: www.dlib.org/dlib/march01/frazier/03frazier.html.

Glasser, Sarah. 2010. "Disappearing Jobs: Staffing Implications for Print Serials Management." *Serials Review* 36, no. 3: 138–146.

Goedeken, Edward A. and Karen Lawson. 2015. "The Past, Present, and Future of Demand-Driven Acquisitions in Academic Libraries." *College & Research Libraries* 76, no. 2: 205–221.

Goodman, Elisabeth and Lucy Loh. 2011. "Organizational Change: A Critical Challenge for Team Effectiveness." *Business Information Review* 28, no. 4: 242–250.

Lopatin, Laurie. 2004. "Review of the Literature: Technical Services Redesign and Reorganization." In *Innovative Redesign and Reorganization of Technical Services: Paths for the Future and Case Studies,* edited by Radford Lee Eden. Westport, CT: Libraries Unlimited.

Morris, Carolyn and Lisa Sibert. 2011. "Acquiring eBooks." In Sue Polanka (ed.). *No Shelf Required: E-Books in Libraries.* Chicago: American Library Association.

NISO. 2010. *The OpenURL Framework for Context-Sensitive Services,* ANSI/ NISO Z39.88-44 (R2010). Baltimore: NISO.

Pesch, Oliver. 2011. "Perfecting COUNTER and SUSHI to Achieve Reliable Usage Analysis." *Serials Librarian* 61, no. 3–4: 353–365.

Pesch, Oliver. 2015. "Implementing SUSHI and COUNTER: A Primer for Librarians." *Serials Librarian* 69, no. 2: 107–125.

Pickett, Carmelita. 2011. "Eliminating Administrative Churn: The 'Big Deal' and Database Subscriptions." *Serials Review* 37, no. 4: 258–261.

Roll, Ann. 2016. "Both Just-In-Time and Just-In-Case: The Demand-Driven-Preferred Approval Plan." *Library Resources & Technical Services* 60, no. 1: 4–11.

Seger, Rebecca and Lenny Allen. 2011. "A Publisher's Perspective on DDA." *Against the Grain* 23, no. 3: 32, 34.

vanDuinkerken, Wyoma, Wendy Arant Kaspar, and Jeanne Harrell. 2014. *Guide to Ethics in Acquisitions.* (ALCTS Acquisitions Guide Series; no. 17.) Chicago: Acquisitions Section of the Association for Library Collections & Technical Services, American Library Association.

CHAPTER FIVE

The Acquisitions Assemblage
Putting It All Together

cquisitions fulfills an essential role in the library, providing access to the myriad resources the library selects and pays for. To successfully support the library's mission, the acquisitions profes sional must master several competencies critical to forming a functional acquisitions assemblage, including: ordering, receiving, establishing access to electronic resources, and processing invoices. Additionally, several related—and intersecting—assemblages must be integrated across these main acquisitions competencies, such as staffing and technology (see chapter 4). In putting all of these components together, a strategic approach to acquisitions can be developed and effectively managed.

Managing Acquisitions

As a strategic piece of library and information assemblages, acquisitions needs to be actively and deliberately managed. To this end, the acquisitions professional must organize many smaller, separate assemblages into the functional acquisitions assemblage. Such assemblages that were previously discussed include:

- Understanding the information ecosystem (resource marketplace)
- Interacting and communicating with personnel (within and outside the library)
- Effectively implementing and integrating technology
- Managing the budget

Regarding this latter point: the flow of acquisitions functions follows a structured (usually annual) cycle determined by the **budget**. The budget defines how much money is available to spend within a given period of time, usually a year. The budget, in turn, is broken into specific **funds**, allocations from the budget for particular expenditures, such as: subject (e.g., history, math, etc.), format (e.g., books, DVDs, etc.), order type (firm order or continuation).

As noted above, this budgetary cycle typically is organized into a twelve-month period for allocating and spending the budget. The fiscal year may coincide with the calendar year, but is typically offset—running, for example, from July 1 to June 30. While spending decisions (i.e., content selection) is typically the purview of collection development, processing the orders for new content, authorizing any renewals for **continuing resources**, and paying the respective invoices before the end of the fiscal year falls to acquisitions. Meeting this ultimate objective of assuring that collection development's content goals are achieved within the mandated budget time frame should be the organizing principle of the acquisitions assemblage.

If the acquisitions assemblage is the strategic means of meeting the library's goals, then the budget is the structure by with which that strategy is framed. The budget determines *how* much is to be spent, while fund allocations focus expenditure on *what* is purchased. Acquisitions generally decides *where* expenditures are made (and perhaps *why*); in collaboration with collection development, acquisitions also determines *who* the library works with to acquire content. Additionally, acquisitions is usually tasked with tracking and carefully documenting expenditures, as well as providing a reliable **audit trail** so that all spent funds are accounted for at the end of the fiscal year.

Alternate Strategies of Access

Content realignments often pose various challenges to acquisitions, especially any practice based in a traditional paradigm. Not all access to content provided by libraries is managed directly by the acquisitions unit or librarian; much of this other content is made available through the library through alternate procurement channels or even provided without cost for the content itself. However, strategies used to provide access through alternate assemblages frequently intersects at one or more points with the acquisitions assemblage.

Local and rare content may not be available through the usual library vendors and may involve additional units of the library, such as special collections or even the administration. Acquisition of local or rare content may involve cultivating local contacts that are not traditional vendors, and providing access to material may involve actually picking material up in person. Local content may include that produced by campus departments, municipal historical societies, or regional auction houses, among many other possible sources not likely to be handled by a commercial vendor. Rare materials might come from such different sources as specialized dealers or online auctions; the complexities in cases of rare materials come not only from rareness (the difficulty to find due to age, limited production, or both), but also from the unique properties of the rare object—the inherent worth of the "content-as-object." In both of these cases—local and rare material—archival considerations are likely to be of major concern, as well.

Working with a consortium (or several consortia) for access often provides opportunities for deep discounting and centralized licensing, which can be a significant benefit to libraries. The opportunity for the vendor or publisher to sell to multiple sites in a single deal can be a major incentive to the seller, as well, and actually position the consortium as a de facto agent for the publishers that it partners with. However, working with a consortium adds an administrative layer for individual libraries that sometimes results in additional work for acquisitions, whether or not the library is working with a vendor or serial agent in addition to the consortium for the purposes of invoicing and access. For example, if a consortium has negotiated a significant discount on a major journals package but has problems billing efficiently, it may be in a library's best interest to subscribe through their preferred subscription agent. Conversely, even if an agent provides timely invoicing and a well-organized online subscription management interface, such services may not be enough to turn down the deep discounting achieved by a consortium. Or, the acquisition and access to content may be centrally managed by the consortial administration and not involve local acquisitions professionals at all. In any case, consortial opportunities and obligations can be a major strategic consideration in sourcing content, particularly resources that have a recurring annual cost.

Open access (OA) is a growing movement to make critical research, especially government or other publicly funded research, available online free of charge. Momentum for the movement has been fueled by the perception of unfair or egregious pricing, particularly of research journals by commercial publishers. When high-profile journals are made available freely online, such as the Public Library of Science (PLoS) (www.plos .org), it is sometimes difficult to determine whether the resource is being acquired or if it is functionally just another free Internet resource being managed in the context of the collection. With no tangible piece to obtain and no invoice to pay, the access can be determined and periodically checked by the collection development department; access can be provided through the Integrated Library System by cataloging. Acquisitions may act on an OA title by managing access or coordinating updates of metadata with the cataloging unit; however, if the journal is added to some content management system, such as a link resolver or discovery service (see chapter 3), access management may well fall to acquisitions. Given the ongoing questions concerning the long-term impact and ultimate role of OA publishing, it may be some time before this category of publication can be comprehensively incorporated into an acquisitions assemblage.

Within the library itself, the licensing of materials has created various possibilities and degrees of access that are far more context- and content-specific than ever before. Sometimes licensed access is tied to print, though more often it is not. What becomes critical in this complex world of information interaction is clearly identifying what the library community needs to access and knowing (or correctly anticipating) what uses the content will be subject to once access is achieved by a user. A priority has also arisen for acquisitions, like the rest of the library, to meet content needs in real time. Acquisitions practitioners must be prepared to facilitate access to content whether it is in a traditional form or not.

Acquisitions practice, like all areas of library work, has been changed by the growing amount, acceptance, expectation, and usage of electronic-based media. Acquisitions has functioned mostly as a reactive practice over time: one where practitioners struggle to keep up with a proliferation of resources, agreements, and content management technologies by absorbing new kinds of content and practice into existing processes and workflows. This reactive practice has, at times, marginalized the practice of acquisitions within the library. While the paradigm dominated by the physical item made acquisitions as much about getting things as obtaining access (the two practices were often the same, or at least conflated), navigation of information sources and formats has grown increasingly complex. The core competencies of ordering, receiving, providing access, and paying for content are no longer comprised principally of clerical practices; while some processes remain paper based, many do not. Redundancy of format, propriety software, nontraditional use of content, and proliferation of access points have all combined, with other challenges, to change the way acquisitions is done, and therefore the way that acquisitions should be thought about. Confusion, frustration, and inefficiency occur when the new imperatives to create a more complex assemblage of access are imposed on a process focused on purchasing physical items. Acquisitions must play a role that emphasizes the strategic, legitimate, and ethical appropriation of content over the mechanical process whereby items are procured.

Archives: Present and Future

The archive is and, especially, was a place for keeping things. Even more than the usual library stacks, the archive was a place where the physical item went to be organized and, above all, preserved. Beyond books, the archive is a place for a varied mix of information objects, such as documents, papers, ephemera, and even realia—that is, actual objects from everyday life (such as chairs, pens, etc.). Because it has been a place that defies conventional collecting practices, the archive has remained largely independent of the conventional acquisitions workflow: it is an assemblage all to itself, where a given object, independent of any content it may record, is frequently important as an artifact. Often, the acquisition of materials for the archive is made under the auspices of an archivist or special collections librarian. Occasionally, acquisitions will support part or even all of the process; in that case, special handling may be required as objects may be one of a kind.

This exceptional workflow makes sense to a certain degree. If acquisitions is process oriented and the process is based on physical items, then the standardization of both the items and the process results in a smooth, even, and, above all, efficient flow of materials. Items destined for the archive are by definition exceptional. Like books, the archive is not going to disappear, become less important, or cease to encompass physical items. But like the book, the archive needs to be reconsidered vis-à-vis acquisitions.

Preservation has always been an element of collection building in libraries. Preservation plays a role in all aspects of the library's collection, from the books in the stacks to the materials in the archive. And acquisitions has always had a role to play in the long-term preservation of materials: specifically, the evaluation and handling of incoming new materials, as well as the replacement of damaged or lost items previously added to the collections.

The reconceptualization of both archival practice and the role that acquisitions plays in preservation needs to come from an improved understanding of the information universe and a better sense of how the idea of format must operate separately from the idea of the item. Preservation can be thought of as a practice and the archive can be thought of as a place. While both have practical implications for the act of acquisition, neither concept provides a way of theorizing the process of acquisition.

When developing an acquisitions strategy, the key is to understand and develop an archival trajectory. That is, rather than relying on a reactive practice of preserving items or the place where items are stored, charting instead an archival trajectory by acquiring formats in a way that meets the anticipated long-term needs of the collections and library users. Following along—and through with—such a trajectory, like many aspects of service, requires close collaboration with other units within the library and its community of users. In a practical sense, the notion of an archival trajectory is not new: content is routinely acquired with particular end uses or end users in mind. However, if acquisitions participates in the process of determining and following the archival trajectory, it is possible to effect a positive impact on library practice. Where acquisitions is formally tasked to collaborate in the determination and projected use of content objects, a richer information environment may be created.

It is possible, though unlikely to be practical, that the object of acquisition for the archive would be handled by acquisitions. This is due to a key difference in the trajectory of the archive versus the general collection. The objects added to the archive tend to be singular in nature with an intrinsic worth that is only partially related to them as objects. More often than not, it is the contingencies surrounding that object—a special edition, a significant signature, a noteworthy owner—anything that sets one object apart from other, ostensibly similar objects and imbues it with singular value. Like acquiring a piece of art, the intrinsic uniqueness of a given item destined for the archive often makes the acquisition of such an object difficult to do separately from its identification and preservation. This is because the archival item is inherently conditional: The identification, acquisition, and preservation all depend on the conditions specific to a singular item. However, acquisitions will likely play an increasing role with archival material, such as the digital backups for electronic formats included in many purchases. In cases where access is mediated by acquisitions, such a role is vital to make sure that content is delivered and stored correctly. The exact nature of the role is highly contingent on the publisher, the content, the intended use, and long-term needs, among other variables.

In those cases where acquisitions is working with and for the archive, format and container will once again overlap. Information objects will also be artifacts. The singularity possessed by these items will make them rare and exceptional, and that has implications for acquiring them. For one, identifying if an item is available and where it might be found (not to mention at what price) may take additional time. Also, such rarities are not likely to be available through mainstream library vendors. A host of online sources and resources can make the job easier but are, again, exceptional even by contemporary acquisitions standards and may involve extensive personal communication and the highest standards of verification that the material is what was represented. For books, local dealers may have something on hand or know how to get it. More likely than not, however, such rarities are not locally procurable. Specialty Web sellers, such seller networks and online storefronts accessible via Amazon or eBay, can provide a quick overview of availability and price. For specialty items, especially those items that are not books, casting a wide net through third-party sellers may be the best approach. Though some of these routes are familiar to many acquisitions practitioners through their personal experience, it is essential to remember that extra consideration may be required when purchasing library content from these sites.

Besides price, however, such purchases conceal some hidden costs. Time invested in searching, placing orders, and evaluating materials upon arrival can be considerable. Especially given that some descriptions online may be less than forthcoming about critical defects to an object, the library takes on some risk purchasing these materials sight unseen; return policies from Web vendors can vary greatly, from the very accommodating to the nonexistent. Shipping and handling costs of such materials may be quite high, and might go even higher if the material needs to be insured—which is almost always an additional cost, when an option at all. In the end, the library may need to track down and purchase a second item, if that is an option, when the condition or bottom-line price of the first item falls outside the acceptable parameters for the library.

One of the most engaging aspects of acquisitions is working with rare, unique, or other special materials. Such acquisitions require some planning before starting out and a solid grasp of what is being sought for the collection, especially the archival trajectory for such items. In this case, the information object becomes a unique artifact where the medium, so to speak, is the message. The item itself may be rare or even irreplaceable. While searching for elusive items may be a rewarding process for the acquisitions professional, the full institutional cost in terms of time and money for such a transaction needs to be taken into account.

"Free": Costs and Considerations

Acquisitions is typically associated with the purchasing of materials. This makes sense, since libraries typically must pay for the information that they provide access to. However, the association of acquisitions only with the processing of paid orders reduces the acquisitions function to something rote and clerical, and diminishes the strategic potential of the acquisitions practitioner in perceived or real terms.

Any academic acquisitions operation interacts with free material in at least several arenas. The notion of the term "free" here mitigates the perceived impact that these interactions actually have. Four common areas of encounter with free materials are gifts or donated materials, open-access publications, locally produced content, and exchange programs. While constituting a small portion of the information universe, these materials may have a disproportionate draw on staff time and resources and must be accounted for in terms of personnel, computing, and storage. Including these categories of free content in the conceptualization of the acquisitions function requires a different kind of thinking.

Materials that come in as random donations can take considerable time to manage. Such random donations may or may not be accepted by the library, then may or may not go to acquisitions. The costs need to be carefully considered; processing content will take time, and storing the content, regardless of its format, will take up space of some kind. Even the opportunity cost—what does not get done at the expense of acting on the free content—should be a factor in deciding what to add. Finally, access to any content will need to be managed for the long term. If it is not feasible to provide systematic and stable access to a particular information object, it is probably better not to act on it. Like all aspects of acquisitions work, any consideration given to such gifts should be part of a broader strategy for actively managing the library's sphere of access. As with other content to which the library wishes to provide access, an acquisitions strategy developed for donations needs to be part of a wider content development program. It is also worthwhile to note that not everything that comes in without an order is a donation. Sometimes unscrupulous publishers will send content that was not ordered in hopes of being able to invoice for it at a later time. Occasionally, an invoice will be included in hopes of tricking the person receiving content at the library into paying for something that was not formally selected.

The OA movement (see above) has gained momentum in recent years and has some uncertain implications for both the publishing and library worlds. Content available on the Web as an OA resource will not be acquired the same way that a paid resource would be. However, if such a resource is intentionally brought into the library's sphere of access, the resource could potentially impact acquisitions. For example, the availability of an OA resource might result in the cancellation of a print publication. While the OA title would not necessarily need to be acquired, the print title would still need to be canceled with the vendor. Acquisitions may also have to manage part of the library's access as a matter of routine e-resource maintenance.

Other routes are available to differently utilize resources in a way that expands the library's sphere of access to various kinds of materials. One such route is through an **exchange program**, where the library trades some material (e.g., duplicate items or locally published content) for other content that may be difficult to otherwise locate or pay for. This can be an effective strategy for dealing with countries or regions where publishing is inconsistent, where lack of infrastructure poses barriers to long-distance business, or the exchange partner has locally produced content that is of interest but not available for sale. Exchanges can also occur between libraries within the same region if they are trying to collect specialized subject content that is generally difficult to obtain. Exchanges, however, can be time-consuming to set up and administer and should be monitored to ensure that the library is getting out of the plan what is being invested in it (Chapman, 2004). Like blanket plans (see chapter 2), exchange programs may be highly rewarding in terms of rare or ephemeral materials, but may require a great deal of time to administer.

Managing eBooks

It is interesting to note that developments in eBooks, on the one hand, and mobile technology, on the other, have brought eBooks into the mainstream. Most significantly, the popularity of mobile devices for reading (such as the Apple iPad and Amazon Kindle) have overcome one of the great challenges in widespread eBook adoption, namely the "e-novel" (or long-form narrative). This flurry of technological innovation and marketing signals a tipping point in the acceptance of eBooks by a growing portion of the general public owning handheld hardware for which digital content objects are being developed. While e-journals in academia, for example, started a major shift from a print-based paradigm to one based both on the production and acceptance of a multiplicity of possible formats, such a shift in popular consumer culture to electronic text suggests an irreversible trend.

Polanka (2011) describes the acquisition and management of eBooks as a "complex labyrinth" (7), citing the numerous challenges that come along with the possibilities offered by the increasing role of eBooks in libraries. Indeed, models of pricing and access continue to proliferate, offering new options while also adding complexity to an already confusing process. For the time being, most models continue to be "hybrids" of sorts, fitting "somewhere between purchasing hard copy items and purchasing electronic subscription items" (Wikoff, 2011: 15). Acquisitions of eBooks often brings management access issues related to both purchasing and subscribing: real-time access and linking issues to the electronic text, on the one hand, while often requiring catalog maintenance and long-term access issues, on the other.

Unlike the eBooks intended for proprietary mobile devices carried by the technologically savvy reading public that mainstream corporations are targeting, the suppliers of academic eBooks have, for the most part, focused their strategy on PC- and laptop-based access. By creating electronic-delivered content, the library is able to take advantage of an increasingly networked wired and wireless infrastructure in public and personal spaces. The library, on the other hand, can capitalize on eBooks as a kind of distributed collection that can be accessed from anywhere, including the physical library itself, homes, classrooms, dorms, and anywhere else with a Wi-Fi and/or cellular signal. Disability services may also be able to leverage computer-delivered content in cases where the digital rights management (DRM) is not too restrictive. Demand in the consumer market for eBooks signals that there may be a similar surge in popularity to follow in academic research. At the same time, research and preservation concerns within the academic community initially resulted in a slower adoption of eBooks in the academic library. Libraries, though, having long dealt with maintaining multiple formats for serials (e.g., print, microform, electronic), are not typically in a position to acquire redundant (through either purchase and/or licensing) monograph content in most cases. This is especially the case for the "new normal" established for many library budgets following the Great Recession. The movement toward e-publishing by mainstream publishers aimed at a general readership has created an atmosphere where eBooks are likely to be more intuitive technologically and more accepted culturally.

The general popularity of eBooks is being driven by many factors including ever-increasing availability, ever-improving technology, accept-able cost, varied pricing and access models, and expansive marketing. In the university, changing research practices and the expectations of incoming students are further driving demand. Popular platforms from both publishers and aggregators (see above) make it possible to integrate eBooks at many points of the selection, acquisition, and discovery processes.

Diminishing Boundaries: The Case of Interlibrary Loan

If acquisitions is increasingly detached from straightforward purchasing and ownership in the strict sense of those terms, while becoming more engaged directly with library users in the process of acquiring content, then the realignment of the acquisitions function clearly spills over its traditional boundaries. If personnel "doing acquisitions" are concerned with maintaining a more generalized and flexible assemblage of access rather than building a tangible physical—that is, "traditional"—collection, other library functions such as interlibrary loan (ILL) and document delivery must be reevaluated within the context of "getting" content and providing access. Though often separated into their own unit or incorporated into access services, a radicalization of acquisitions may well mean a shift in how these less permanent, patron-driven acquisitions are managed within the library. At the very least, approval and DDA plans require close coordination between collection development and acquisitions; however, connecting with content in a complex information ecosystem requires close collaboration with ILL and document delivery operations in addition to collection development.

The idea of *purchase-on-demand* (POD) or *interlibrary loan patron-driven acquisitions* (ILL PDA) is not a new concept, as a review of literature on the topic reveals (Moeller, 2012). Indeed, such an approach may seem a natural synthesis of two increasingly related assemblages within the library. Reighart and Oberlander (2008) observe bluntly that "[p]urchasing books is the most familiar of practices for libraries, and maybe ILL should be doing more of it" (187). However, the transition to such a model may be challenging in practical terms—especially for print content. Significant challenges with employing such a model have included administrative considerations, like workflow and budget concerns (Fountain and Frederiksen, 2010), as well as the possibility of higher transaction cost for ILL DDA versus regular (i.e., non-acquisitive) ILL (van Dyk, 2011). However, with growing availability and acceptance of eBooks, adoption of full DDA plans can help facilitate this change by building fund assignments and user selections directly into the acquisitions workflow. In a matter of time, it may be difficult to maintain sharp distinctions in respective functions of the various "acquisitions" processes to keep them strictly separate.

eBooks, again, provide another interesting example. While a journal article not owned by the library may be supplied through pay-per-view or document delivery service, what about books in an electronic format: do these fall into the bailiwick of ILL? Given the DRM surrounding eBooks, it seems unlikely that many providers will allow loans outside of the institution or institutions (within a state system or consortium) that established access to the title to begin with. Since many eBook publishers already offer patron-driven (or other real-time) acquisitions options, it seems more likely that instead of ILL, libraries may need to (or choose to) satisfy user needs by simply allowing just-in-time purchasing of e-titles in many cases. While budgetary considerations (price per item and overall budget situation) will set de facto limits on patron selection, such a model not only provides immediate access but allows ongoing access for future library users. Developing such a service is clearly part of the acquisitions function: It is just another kind of book purchase. It is unlikely that all ILL and document delivery services will be immediately absorbed by acquisitions, and in many cases such a merge might not even make sense for a myriad of reasons (e.g., organizationally, budgetary, etc.). However, when looking at how information is being produced, distributed, and consumed, an approach to access should not impose distinctions from an old paradigm. eBooks provide an example of a format for which it has become difficult to differentiate anticipatory acquisitions ("just-in-case") from just-in-time delivery. In the Information Age, such a sharp delineation needs to be abandoned in favor of an acquisitions continuum. Instead of silos of content and responsibility, rigid and separate, functional boundaries must be fluid, permeable, and conducive to collaboration across the entire library in order to meet a variety of content needs.

Radical Strategies: Strategic Assemblages

It is an empirical fact that we live in an age of information overload. We are inundated by vast amounts of information: the Internet, cable and satellite television, and satellite radio all feed a continuous stream of information. Cellular and Wi-Fi technology practically ensure ubiquitous connection to the networked world. Constant advances in computing and telecommunications make accessibility to this information at once easier to access, as well as more portable.

Within this environment crowded with information noise, the library—once an undisputed destination for the information seeker—is now one of many nodes among a multiplicity of information streams. To isolate and harness particular information objects, the acquisitions professional must navigate a challenging terrain in the quest for the right information in the most relevant format—then establish the necessary access, whether that is buying a book or licensing a database. Ultimately, the *use* and, therefore, **meaning** of content is highly dependent on a combination of factors—including context and interpretation. As the information ecosystem becomes more complicated, the strategies employed to establish the requisite access to content obviously become more complicated as well. The most difficult part in an environment that is both increasingly complicated and always in flux is to establish a stable, meaningful strategy for acquisitions—as well as the corresponding workflows that form the basis of the acquisitions assemblage.

On the one hand, new technologies provide new tools and opportunities for acquisitions on a continuous basis. On the other hand, the very flux that delivers options for purchase and access also demands that successful strategies be adaptable and, therefore, technology-neutral—at least, to the extent possible. This paradox underlies all the challenges that contemporary practitioners of acquisitions must incorporate into their daily work.

Rather than reconfiguring old approaches to acquisitions—left then only to reconfigure them again—practitioners must radicalize how they approach and perform acquisitions in the Information Age. This is, of course, easier said than done. While the competencies in acquisitions—placing orders, receiving materials or establishing access to resources, paying invoices—are what fundamentally define the practice within each library and across the profession, developing a singular, *localized* acquisitions assemblage remains incredibly important for an effective acquisitions program. The variables that constitute the local also confound any attempt at a fully prescriptive methodology: the particular population(s) served, their specific information needs, the collection focus, staffing levels, facilities, budget, and tax status are just a few variables operating at a local level that create a highly unique acquisitions situation at each library. What becomes obvious is that fixed approaches to acquisitions based on the primacy of paper will become increasingly inadequate to address the complex information needs of library users.

THE ACQUISITIONS ASSEMBLAGE

Core Competencies

- Ordering
- Receiving/Access
- Paying

Local Variables

- Mission
- Collection focus (or foci)
- Content contingencies
- Staffing levels

- Facilities
- Funding source(s)
- Budget
- Tax status

What, then, does it mean to "radicalize" acquisitions? The most important step is to move definitively away from models that are based either (1) on the fixed linearity of process, or (2) the presumed standardization of information objects, pricing models, etc. Process instead should focus proactively on evaluating content options and searching for access solutions. Reflexively buying a book may not be an adequate strategy; engaging with collection development and access services to determine access needs, format availability, and new service models for delivering content to end users regardless of their location is an approach on which to form a basis of acquisitions practice. While this is difficult to do, creatively engaging with the content goals and access issues within the context of a given library environment should inform any acquisitions strategy; service needs should drive acquisitions practices forward.

The use of vendors when possible, technology when effective, and collaboration at each step of the way will leverage resources, streamline workflows, and facilitate appropriate access. In the abstract, these are not new ideas. However, each one of these elements takes on new meaning and greater significance in technology-driven, always-online, interdisciplinary ecosystem. The paradigm has shifted from a modern, mechanical information system to a postmodern ecology that is often networked and nonlinear. In other words, our information, cultural, and technological assemblages have grown more complicated, more interconnected, and less clearly defined than ever before.

The idea of "postmodern acquisitions" is not new, and has been a mode of thinking from early in the Information Age (Propas and Reich, 1995). However, a postmodern praxis within the realm of acquisitions is finally starting to reach its potential because of advances in technology coupled with changes in information-seeking culture. Immersed in this expanding, diversifying information ecosystem, acquisitions professionals now find themselves facing a proliferation of formats—a vast field crowded with Jean Baudrillard's concept of **simulacra**, or copies without originals. Information exists as prints, reprints, photocopies, Web pages, scanned images, CDs, e-mails, streaming video, audio files, tweets, photos, soundbites—a host of formats endlessly migrating and propagating themselves through the environment. Content can be reproduced and remixed across a variety of formats, distributed through an endless number of channels, and acted upon in infinite ways. The role of the original has not disappeared—far from it—but the original in terms of use (and therefore acquisitions) will hold different meanings context to context. So, too, will the role of the item. Though acquisitions professionals will continue to buy items (and continue to contribute to the building of "traditional" collections), the gathering of physical items is just one part of connecting library users with content. The acquisitions professional must not only be aware of or just take into account, but must actively incorporate new kinds of formats, unfamiliar objects, and challenging service models into their daily work.

Conclusion: Rhizomatic Acquisitions

Any acquisitions work today must be premised on an ever-growing amount of information, the ever-changing nature of content and technology, and an ability to be proactive and flexible in building the library's assemblage of access. Deleuze and Guattari provide a fitting model for tracing information and acquiring formats in the new information age: "A system like this could be called a rhizome. A **rhizome** as a subterranean stem is absolutely different from roots and radicles" (1987: 6), typical of plants like ferns or bamboo. Instead of providing a singular position or direction, "there are no points or positions in a rhizome, such as those found in a structure, root, or tree. There are only lines" (8). Rather than fixed categories of content in fixed format traveling along limited, linear chains in predetermined directions, a rhizomatic approach in acquisitions suggests moving in any and all directions to establish, develop, and refine the acquisitions assemblage that allows library users to connect with the content that they seek. Rhizomatic lines represent the shortest routes, yet simultaneously imply free motion and growth throughout the information ecosystem. These lines are multidimensional; rhizomes do *not dig* in but *go outward* in strategic directions.

This break, moving acquisitions from the notion of linear chains of an item-based, collection-focused workflow to the rhizomatic lines of an object-based, user-focused assemblage is not to be underestimated. DeLanda elaborates that in the context of assemblages, "the formula for linear causality, 'Same cause, same effect, always,' has had damaging effects on the very conception of the relations between cause and effect" (19). The apparently linear chains may, in fact, be composed of segments, with each segment in a sense forming a link of the chain that connects author to publisher to vendor to library to user, for example. This connection may end up being a direct one—or not. DeLanda continues that "while rigid habits may be enough to associate linear causes with their effects, they are not enough to deal with nonlinear causes that demand more adaptive, flexible skills" (50–51).

So what seem at the outset to be straightforward linear *chains* may, in fact, may be more than they appear—more complicated, more nuanced, more rhizomatic *lines*. Following Deleuze and Guattari, we are able at this point to "summarize the principal difference between rigid segmentarity and supple segmentarity. In the rigid mode, binary segmentarity stands on its own and is governed by great machines of direct binarization, whereas in the other [that is, *supple*] mode, binaries result from 'multiplicities of n dimensions'" (1987: 212). Deleuze and Guattari, then, recognize the segmentary nature of the rigid lines, but note that they are functionally "governed by great machines of direct binarization." In the case of acquisitions, such "great machines" imposing this binarization might be traditional library practices; organizational rigidity of the unit, library, or parent organization; or even a reluctance to consider new approaches. The end points in these cases of rigid segmentarity have already been pre-established and are connected by fixed, predetermined lines—even if those lines are, in turn, composed of many segments. The flexibility, or suppleness, of the rhizomatic lines grants freedom—in terms of both the length and directionality of the lines. The "multiplicities of n dimensions" are opened up by the expanding number of formats, contingencies, and collaborations, allowing acquisitions to escape its own past limitations and fully emerge into the possibilities of the Information Age.

The radicalization of acquisitions requires the dismantling of the pre-existing conceptual apparatus of acquisitions—a fixed, rooted system—and reconstituting the assemblage as something at once less structured and more connected: "a multiplicity that necessarily changes in nature as it expands its connections" (Deleuze and Guattari, 1987: 8). As the eco-system expands, diversifies, and evolves–and as connections between content, users, and technology increase–routes to access and mechanisms of feedback increase, too. It is difficult to respond to novel user needs and expectations in a truly meaningful way when enmeshed in a fixed system, and even more challenging to meet those needs and expectations in a *proactive* way. Reconceiving the environment as an assemblage (and also *many* assemblages) of varied information, content, and formats, with all that might imply, rather than a rigidly structured system of exclusively physical entities to be bought and shelved—such an ecology, where there are only lines, is the absolute key to assembling acquisitions in the Information Age.

REFERENCES

Baudrillard, Jean. 1994. *Simulacra and Simulation*. Translated by Sheila Faria Glaser. Ann Arbor: University of Michigan Press.

Chapman, Liz. 2004. *Managing Acquisitions in Library and Information Services*, Rev. Ed. London: Facet Publishing.

DeLanda, Manuel. 2006. *A New Philosophy of Society: Assemblage Theory and Social Complexity*. New York: Continuum Books.

Deleuze, Gilles and Felix Guattari. 1987. *A Thousand Plateaus: Capitalism and Schizophrenia*. Minneapolis: University of Minnesota Press.

Fountain, Kathleen Carlisle and Linda Frederiksen. 2010. "Just Passing Through: Patron-Initiated Collection Development in Northwest Academic Libraries." *Collection Management* 35, no. 3/4: 185–195.

Moeller, Paul D. 2012. "Literature of Acquisitions in Review, 2010–11." *Library Resources & Technical Services* 57, no. 2: 87–99.

Polanka, Sue. 2011. "Purchasing eBooks in Libraries: A Maze of Opportunities and Challenges." In Sue Polanka (ed.). *The No Shelf Required Guide to eBook Purchasing: A Library Technology Report*. Chicago: ALA Editions, 4–7.

Propas, Sharon and Vicky Reich. 1995. "Postmodern Acquisitions." *Library Acquisitions: Practice and Theory* 19, no. 1: 43–48.

Reighart, Renee and Cyril Oberlander. 2008. "Exploring the Future of Interlibrary Loan: Generalizing the Experience of the University of Virginia, USA." *Interlending & Document Supply* 36, no. 4: 184–190.

van Dyk, Garrit. 2011. "Interlibrary Loan Purchase-on-Demand: A Misleading Literature." *Library Collections, Acquisitions, & Technical Services* 35, no. 2/3: 83–89.

Wikoff, Karin. 2011. *Electronic Resources Management in the Academic Library: A Professional Guide*. Oxford: ABC-CLIO.

APPENDIX

Code of Ethics
of the American
Library Association

As members of the American Library Association, we recognize the importance of codifying and making known to the profession and to the general public the ethical principles that guide the work of librarians, other professionals providing information services, library trustees and library staffs.

Ethical dilemmas occur when values are in conflict. The American Library Association Code of Ethics states the values to which we are committed, and embodies the ethical responsibilities of the profession in this changing information environment.

We significantly influence or control the selection, organization, preservation, and dissemination of information. In a political system grounded in an informed citizenry, we are members of a profession explicitly committed to intellectual freedom and the freedom of access to information. We have a special obligation to ensure the free flow of information and ideas to present and future generations.

The principles of this Code are expressed in broad statements to guide ethical decision making. These statements provide a framework; they cannot and do not dictate conduct to cover particular situations.

I. We provide the highest level of service to all library users through appropriate and usefully organized resources; equitable service policies; equitable access; and accurate, unbiased, and courteous responses to all requests.

II. We uphold the principles of intellectual freedom and resist all efforts to censor library resources.

III. We protect each library user's right to privacy and confidentiality with respect to information sought or received and resources consulted, borrowed, acquired or transmitted.

IV. We respect intellectual property rights and advocate balance between the interests of information users and rights holders.

V. We treat co-workers and other colleagues with respect, fairness, and good faith, and advocate conditions of employment that safeguard the rights and welfare of all employees of our institutions.

VI. We do not advance private interests at the expense of library users, colleagues, or our employing institutions.

VII. We distinguish between our personal convictions and professional duties and do not allow our personal beliefs to interfere with fair representation of the aims of our institutions or the provision of access to their information resources.

VIII. We strive for excellence in the profession by maintaining and enhancing our own knowledge and skills, by encouraging the professional development of co-workers, and by fostering the aspirations of potential members of the profession.

Adopted at the 1939 Midwinter Meeting by the ALA Council; amended June 30, 1981; June 28, 1995; and January 22, 2008.

■ ■ ■

Available: www.ala.org/advocacy/proethics/codeofethics/codeethics

Glossary

A-toZ list. An alphabetical and hyperlinked list of a library's electronic journal and/or database titles.

acquisitions. The strategic and ethical appropriation of paid content for the library **collection.**

agent. *See* **subscription agent.**

applied ethics. Putting principles of "right action," or **ethics,** into practice.

approval plan. A vendor service where filtered title notifications or pre-selected books are supplied to the library automatically according to an established **profile.** Books may have received **physical processing** by the **jobber** prior to shipment.

assemblage. A whole, comprised of separate parts, that gains irreducible properties from the interaction between the parts of which it is composed. The parts themselves may actually be assemblages themselves, made up of other parts. The whole, in turn, may be part of a larger assemblage.

budget. Amount of available money.

code. A collection of principles or guiding statements.

collection. The pool of resources legitimately available to library users.

collection development. The formal process of selecting content available to a library's user community.

consortium (pl. *consortia*). A group of libraries working together as a collective entity, often to leverage a discount on resource acquisition (especially e-resources).

content. Information that can be communicated.

contingency. Considerations that relate uniquely to a particular type of content object.

continuing resources. Resources paid on an ongoing basis, such as subscriptions and electronic content with access fees.

continuation. A serial that is published irregularly or occasionally.

digital rights management (DRM). Embedded code that restricts use (especially duplication and transmission) of digital content.

discovery. Context where content is found both intentionally and serendipitously.

discovery layer. *See* **discovery service.**

discovery service. An integrating Web-scale search technology that brings together disparate library-provided resources. Also called a **discovery layer.**

drop ship. When a vendor has a physical item sent directly from the publisher because the ordered item is not in stock. Material is still invoiced through the vendor.

eBook. A text that is entirely available in electronic form. May be "born digital" or not.

EBA. *See* **evidence-based acquisitions.**

EDI. *See* **electronic data interchange.**

electronic data interchange (EDI). A protocol for the electronic transmission of information. Libraries may be able to set up EDI for ordering, invoicing, or even claiming missing content from vendors through the ILS. Two common EDI standards used within the library environment are EDIFACT and X12.

encumbrance. Funds reserved (or *encumbered*) and tracked for an anticipated payment that have not yet been paid to a seller (i.e., expended).

ethics. Actions that are right.

evidence based acquisitions (EBA). Plan with a publisher where an agreed-to budget amount is spent on a subset of available eBooks after a period of demonstrated use.

exchange program. A program set up between two or more libraries where content is traded among participants.

firm order. Commitment to acquire a single thing (e.g., book, DVD, etc.).

format. The technological means used to both inscribe and transmit content.

fugitive literature. *See* gray literature.

funds. Allocations from the **budget** designated for specific purposes (e.g., particular subject areas).

gray literature. Content produced and distributed outside mainstream publication channels, and may therefore be difficult to acquire systematically. Such content will likely be most important to research, special, or technical libraries.

information. Anything that can be known.

Information Age. Period of time in which a discourse or paradigm centered on the abundance, distribution, and use of information, and its corresponding social, political, and economic value remains sustained.

information ecosystem. The environment where elements of information— production, distribution, consumption, discussion, and modification— simultaneously interact.

item. A physical thing.

jobber. Traditional term for a book **vendor.**

knowledgebase (KB). A large index of all potentially available electronic content, where a library centrally manages access to its specific acquired content.

license. A contract setting out terms for use and access of (especially electronic) content.

link resolver. Technology based on the OpenURL format used to mediate user searches and identify the requested content from one or more sources.

local content. Content that has been produced locally and may have limited distribution or relevance. A newsletter from a local historical society or video of a town hall meeting are examples of local content.

material. Having perceptible and tangible form.

monograph. A single, complete (usually textual) work published as an integrated whole.

meaning. Significance bestowed by knowledge, context, and interpretation.

object. Particular content existing in a particular format.

open access (OA). At its most basic, the OA movement is about removing barriers to information access by making research available free online. Advocates for OA are found among librarians, researchers, legislators, and publishers. A major objective is to make content, especially published journal articles based on publicly funded research, as widely available and easily accessible as possible. This is in part a reaction to increasing serial pricing, diminishing library budgets, economic inequality, and other barriers to access.

OpenURL. Used to facilitate linking to any relevant sources (including full text and catalog records) where requested content can be accessed by an authorized library user.

p-card. A credit card issued by the university for university-related purchasing.

paradigm. Coherent system of thought and perception.

perpetual access. Licensed access granted by a publisher "in perpetuity" (i.e., forever) to electronic content.

physical processing. Preparing an item for library use. Such processing might include any combination of bar coding, property stamping, adding security devices, inserting bookplates, covering, or binding. Vendors may offer services where they will process items on behalf of the library for a fee, often as part of an **approval plan.**

profile. The often elaborate criteria by which the vendor supplies pre-selected notifications or content to the library on an automatic basis.

publish. To formally prepare content and make it publically available.

rare content. Content that is difficult to access. Though the typical example of a rare content object is a rare book, rare content might also include sites from the "hidden" or "Deep" Web, or electronic content contained in an obsolete format. Rare content is often more challenging to obtain than other content and may have contingencies regarding access or long-term preservation. Content stored in an obsolete format, such as BetaMax tapes or floppy discs, may require likewise obsolete (i.e., hard to find and/or use) hardware to access the content.

request for proposal (RFP). A process by which the library requests bids from vendors as part of a formal selection process. Besides volume and price of items, the RFP usually indicates other service requirements, such as shipping costs, processing specifications, and anything else related to the provision of content to the library. The successful bid is typically awarded a contract for a fixed amount of time (e.g., 3 or 5 years).

RFP. *See* **request for proposal.**

rhizome. A subterranean stem, as opposed to roots; used by Delueze to describe a model based on multidirectionality and segmentation.

serial. A work of indefinite or ongoing duration, such as a journal or a newspaper.

series. A work of defined scope but indefinite duration, such as a publisher's topical series.

set. A work released in parts but considered finite in scope and duration, such as an encyclopedia. (Also called a *terminal set* because it covers a finite topic and has an anticipated end point.)

sharp practice. Gaining advantage through unscrupulous behavior.

shelf-ready. Items that are completely physically processed by a vendor to be ready for shelving as soon as the items are checked in at the library, usually as part of an **approval plan**.

simulacrum (pl. *simulacra*). A copy without an original.

sole source justification. A documented circumstance in which certain content and/or service(s) are available only from a single provider.

standing order. Commitment to acquire all the content in a **set, series,** or **continuation.**

subscription. Commitment to acquire on a recurring basis all the issues published in a defined period, usually one year.

subscription agent. Term for a vendor of serials and periodicals, and related services.

terminal set. *See* **set.**

theory. A unified way of describing, organizing, and planning professional work.

vendor. A third-party entity that resells, licenses, or aggregates published content. May also provide related technology and/or services. (*See also* **jobber** and **subscription agent.**)

Web-scale. At the scale of the World Wide Web.

Index